.12.17

ע

ינ

A Long Way from Home

The wartime experiences of a small
boy evacuated from East Sussex to
West Yorkshire in 1939

ALASTAIR TOMPKINS

Woodfield

Woodfield Publishing Ltd

Bognor Regis ~ West Sussex ~ England ~ PO21 5EL
tel 01243 821234 ~ **e/m** info@woodfieldpublishing.co.uk

Interesting and informative books on a variety of subjects

For full details of all our published titles, visit our website at
www.woodfieldpublishing.co.uk

7453

To Pauline

~ CONTENTS ~

Prologue

During the last sixty years we have lived at peace. Prior to this period the world had been ravaged by two wars. The year 1914 commenced with Germany invading Belgium. Having crushed her small army, Germany now attacked her old enemy, France. British troops were sent to assist in her defence. Before this war ended in 1918 with Germany's defeat, millions of men on both sides had died in the carnage of what became known as the 'Western Front'. Thousands of girls in Britain were to remain single for the rest of their lives as their sweethearts lay buried within the soil of France.

The peace that followed was short lived; just twenty-one years. The Allies had agreed at the Treaty of Versailles that Germany could once again, with restrictions, re-arm. For example, in order to maintain the might of the British navy with its sixteen-inch guns, Germany was restricted to thirteen-inch guns and its battleships were to be restricted in size. This 'inferior' navy was referred to as *'pocket battleships'*. This agreement would prove to be a huge mistake.

Germany was still smarting at their defeat. Under their new leader, Hitler, an anti-Semitic fervour was encouraged; their army was enlarged; teenagers joined the 'Hitler Youth'; massed rallies were held and the new German flag, the 'Swastika', was displayed on public buildings. Now being permitted by the Allies to re-arm, their factories commenced to produce war materials. By 1939 Germany was poised once again to plunge Europe into war. The first move was to annex Austria. The Allies watched but 'sat on their hands'. Britain was ill-prepared to meet this growing threat. Some preparations were made. The Territorial Army was readied to be mobilised. As Germany had used toxic gas during 1914-1918, gas-masks were issued to the entire population.

Germany was now poised to attack Poland. Britain had a treaty with Poland. When the German attack came we declared war on Germany and we sent troops to France to 'hold the line'.

Germany had learned many lessons from the 1914-18 war. Due to trench warfare, mass assaults by infantry against shells and machine-gun fire had cost both sides many millions of lives. Germany had now developed '*Blitz Krieg*' – aerial bombardment ahead of mass attacks by tanks followed by infantry. Faced with this onslaught the Allied armies reeled under its impact. Within a very short space of time Europe would be over-run. The battered British army retreated; many in the French army threw away their arms and deserted, leaving their flanks exposed to the advancing enemy. The British now held a perimeter around the beaches of Dunkirk. Despite being attacked by a superior force by land and air, the perimeter was held. Due to this spirited defence, many thousands of men were rescued and returned to defend our shores – leaving on the roads of France and the beaches of Dunkirk masses of weaponry and essential supplies.

Across the English Channel we now faced a triumphant, well armed German army poised to invade. Two aircraft, the Supermarine '*Spitfire*' and the Hawker '*Hurricane*', piloted by young men with little experience of aerial combat faced superior odds. If they failed to win this forthcoming aerial battle, Germany could invade and Britain, like Europe, would be 'under the German heel'. Later Winston Churchill stated: "*Never in the field of human conflict was so much owed by so many to so few".* These gallant fighter pilots, backed by the Royal Navy and our defeated army, was all that we had to defend our country. It is against this background that this true story about a very young boy emerges.

Alastair Tompkins
Crowthorne, Berkshire
November 2013

1. The storm clouds gather

The year was 1939. It had been a long, hot summer. Each day was idyllic and the village of Polegate in East Sussex had much to offer. With my friend Peter, who was also five, we had used our hands to catch newts in the local pond, taking home our catch in washed out jam jars. Then, when the poor creatures failed to survive, we dug graves and buried them with due reverence, marking each one with twigs tied in the shape of a cross. We had walked on the local Downs, sustained by water carried in empty lemonade bottles and jam and cheese sandwiches provided by our respective larders. We had visited the derelict 'haunted house' – and had 'run for our lives' when we heard a strange noise that was, no doubt, some peeling wallpaper stirring in the breeze, or some field mouse scampering amidst the ruins. To our child-like ears it was a ghost!

Next to our house was a large open field. This provided a 'playground', not only for Peter and me but other children of a similar age. The addition of several sheets of corrugated iron left by the builders the previous year, provided the basic major material for building camps, dens and a place to play 'mothers and fathers'- which was particularly favoured by the blonde-haired girl who lived next door. Not only did our dens have a roof but, due to the number of corrugated sheets, it was also possible to construct three 'rooms'!

During school time, Peter and I followed a basic routine. Every morning my mother, or grandmother, would provide me with a small pat of butter wrapped in grease-proof paper and a penny. On my way to school I would call for Peter who was similarly provided. Our route was: at the end of the road turn right; walk up the village street – passing to our right the public house where the father of one of our friends was the publican – up to the 'T' junction, cross the road to the village bakery, and with our respective pennies purchase a hot crusty bread roll. We would then exit the shop, turn right and each clutching our paper bags, walk along the road until we arrived opposite the school entrance, then carefully cross the road and enter the low school gate. Before our lessons commenced there was time to meet other boys; perhaps haggle over 'swops', or boast how brave we had been when confronting a ghost at the derelict 'haunted' house. These activities would be interrupted by the School Mistress appearing at the school entrance and ringing a small hand-bell. I can recall that she was slim; had a kindly face; was not very pretty; her hair was worn close to her head in a series of deeply crimped waves and that she wore small, round silver-framed glasses.

Each morning, just prior to break-time, we would line up as our School Mistress handed each child a small bottle with a waxed cap containing a third of a pint of milk, plus a straw. In the centre of the waxed cap was a small indentation that could be pushed down and the drinking straw inserted. Returning to our desks to consume our daily issue, out would come the now cool crusty bread roll. The roll would be broken open, the small pat of butter would be spread with our fingers, and our teeth would sink into its delicious smelling crusty surface, then down into the generous layer of butter 'buried' deep inside its soft interior. The straws provided a daily game. With the final few drops of milk residing in the base of the bottle, a hard suck on the straw produced a series of loud, rude noises. With several children, mostly boys, trying to outdo each other, the volume of noise had to be heard to be believed!

Break times were always popular. The more rough and tumble games of 'tag' or marbles were conducted by the boys, with 'hopscotch' and skipping ropes being used by the girls – who never failed to say "We'll tell teacher" when our game of 'tag' intruded into their more genteel pastimes. Repeated intrusion could even result in a screwed-up face and having a tongue pointed in our direction, which concluded with the words, "so there!" In those days of innocence we knew that girls, although the same shape as ourselves, were not really like boys. There were major differences for all to see. They played sissy games; were, we had to admit, prettier than ourselves; cried easily if they were bumped into and, unlike us, they couldn't climb trees.

Each week I received pocket money – a whole silver sixpence. This princely sum was sufficient to purchase a bar of 'Fry's' chocolate cream, or perhaps even better, a bar of 'Cadburys' chocolate filled with strawberry cream fondant. This still left four whole pennies to last the remainder of the week! Peter received a similar sum and with our 'savings' sometimes on our way home from school we would again visit the bakery to purchase two pennies-worth of stale cakes. These were cakes that had not sold the previous day and, depending on the residual stock, it was possible to receive as many as four differ-ent cakes. Doughnuts with jam centres; jam tarts; currant buns; custard tarts and sometimes a chocolate éclair! From these bags of 'child's dreams' we would select and consume our favourites, taking the balance to school next day to swop for marbles or some other 'priceless' item that had been removed from a pocket and shown to an admiring group, who would draw in breath and give advice as to its value.

"Cor a brass button off a soldier's coat! I wouldn't swop it for a jam tart." However, to a five-year-old boy, the sight of a strawberry jam tart so close to his nose that he could smell it, was difficult to resist. Now had it been a currant bun, the ultimate sum to secure this 'priceless' object could mean the addition of a half-penny or 'ha'penny'. Other sales were less protracted. A stale custard tart would be accepted with alacrity and a whole penny would be slipped into the left-hand pocket of my grey flannel shorts – the right-hand pocket being reserved for a carefully folded and ironed white cotton handkerchief.

This basic altruistic approach was not always possible. The reason was a rather large bar of chocolate called 'Double Six'. Let me explain. This bar was at least three times the size of my normal tuppenny bar and contained twelve centres, each pair of centres filled with different tasting coloured fondants, which included my two favourites, peppermint and strawberry. To enter the sweet-shop at the bottom of our road clutching my sixpence, and seeing bars of 'Double Six' staring me in the face, coupled with very strong recalls of their delicious varied centres, with thoughts of stale cakes, plus 'swops' for marbles and other 'fabulous' items fighting for dominance, I have to admit that the lure of a whole bar of 'Double Six' often won.

Peter's father worked for another bakery some miles away. From time to time we would be invited to sit beside him in his 'Morris' van to visit the bakery where dough was being pounded by hand, sliced with sharp knives, flipped onto a scale, then the resultant lump placed into a tin prior to being fed into the series of large ovens. The bakers, mostly men, wearing small round cotton hats and matching white aprons, would have forearms covered in flour and, with the heat from the ovens, plus their exertions – beads of sweat gathered on their foreheads as they pounded and kneaded large lumps of warm dough. My favourite was the 'cottage loaf', so called due to its unusual shape. A baker would slice off a lump of warm dough, then mould it into a ball about six inches across and smack it down onto the flour-covered wooden table. He would then cut off a second smaller slice of dough and again mould this into a ball, then dipping his fingers into a small basin of water, wet one side and press it onto the larger ball. Finally, using a finger, he would put a small hollow in the top. This final act always impressed me as it confirmed what my grandmother had told me when I asked why I had a belly button. She said: "When babies are ready to enter the world, God came along to check each one. To do this he would poke his finger onto the belly of each baby to test it, nodding to himself with satisfaction as he walked down the line saying, "You're done, and you're done." I can recall asking about black babies? My grandmother was never lost for an answer. "This is because they have been baked for longer and brown babies for a little longer than white ones." This adult knowledge about babies and belly buttons more than satisfied my childlike curiosity. However, some months later a moment of confusion arose when my Aunt Lucy informed me in answer to my grow-ing level of interest: "babies were found under gooseberry bushes." When I posed the question about their belly buttons, my Aunt informed me that the Angels placed the babies under gooseberry bushes after God had checked them. The mere fact that far-off lands didn't have gooseberry bushes was to me an unknown factor, so yet again my childish curiosity was more than satisfied.

One day I called at Peter's house to be met at the door by his father dressed in a khaki army uniform, which had a high button collar, breast and side pockets, numerous brass buttons and below the knees, wide khaki 'bandages' wound round and round each leg, stopping at a pair of very shiny black boots. Peter appeared at his father's side.

"My Dad's in the Territorial Army and has to go away."

He reached for his father's hand and was rewarded by having his hair ruffled. Peter's mother then appeared looking pale and, due to her puffy eyes, I realised she had been crying.

"Where are you going?" I asked. My hair was also ruffled.

"I'm off to camp" came the reply which caused Peter's mother to dab her eyes with her flower-patterned apron. She bent down and spoke to me.

"Alastair, Peter isn't coming out to play today, so be a good boy. You run along home and you can see Peter tomorrow."

I walked down the garden path and set off towards our house. Why was Peter's mother crying? Camps were exciting and being a soldier even more exciting!

Arriving home I entered the back door to find my grandmother in the kitchen preparing some food. "You're back early," she remarked as I sat down on the opposite side of the wooden kitchen table.

"Yes, grandma, Peter's mother was crying because his Dad is off to camp with the army. It can't be for long and he was looking very smart in his uniform."

My grandmother put down her small peeling knife and patted her lap.

"Come and give me a cuddle."

I settled onto her lap as her warm arms enveloped me and she planted a gentle kiss on my forehead.

"There are some nasty people in the world called 'Germans' and Peter's father, with his comrades, will ensure that they do not do any more nasty things."

"What sort of nasty things grandma?"

My grandmother held me a little closer and rocked slightly backwards and forwards. I looked up into her face to see that her eyes were filled with tears.

"Grandma, don't cry, if they come here and do nasty things I'll fight them!"

At this early age I did not know that her son, Victor, aged just eighteen, had been killed in the final month of the First World War that had ended just twenty-one years previously, or that some of my Aunts had never married as their sweethearts had failed to return from the carnage that was the graveyard of millions, The Western Front.

Peter and I continued to roam around and one day found an army camp situated beside a wood very close to the Downs. There were neat lines of conical-shaped tents, and smoke was rising from a two-wheeled cart. As we drew closer it became obvious it was for cooking. A soldier dressed in a round-necked khaki shirt and off- white braces, called us over.

"You boys hungry? Here have this." And he handed us a warm loaf of bread which we carried off into the woods. We sat down and tore off lumps of this delicious warm bread which, we were sure, was the best that we had ever tasted. Some weeks later we returned to the same spot. It was devoid of any signs of the army. They had gone.

The school holidays were coming to a close. Six of us, including Peter and our friend from the local pub, decided that it was time for adventure! Following numerous suggestions – and several boasts of how far we could walk in a day – we settled on walking to Eastbourne. When should we go? As it was still early in the day there was no time like the present. Armed with a loaf of crusty bread and a large bottle of lemonade purchased with our pooled funds, and only a vague idea of how to get there, we set off in the general direction of Eastbourne, little realising what a panic our unannounced departure would cause.

Now, for a group of young boys, the six or seven miles were proving to be somewhat arduous, but we were determined to get to Eastbourne and our enthusiasm soon dispelled the fears of the faint-hearted. At around two o'clock we arrived at the entrance to a park, tired and footsore. We had arrived! There ahead of us was a large pond with at least ten model sailing boats being sailed backwards and forwards by their proud, grey-haired owners. What more could six boys want? We settled down on the close-cut grass beside the pond and carefully shared out our meagre rations as we continued to watch the spectacle with great interest.

We didn't have a watch between us, but as the majority of the boat owners were removing their boats from the water, it was agreed that it was time to head for home. Still tired and foot-sore, with numerous stops to rest, we somehow lost our way. Where were we? By now it was dusk and we were walking along a country lane with one member of our party openly sobbing as he was fully convinced he would never see his mother again. Darkness fell and as we only had on our daytime clothing, we were starting to feel chilly. With sore feet we continued along the lane having decided that if we came upon a house we would call and ask for directions.

Some minutes later we could see the headlights of an ap-proaching car. We decided that we'd stop it and ask for directions. It stopped about six feet away illuminating us in its headlights. We heard a door open and a tall, burly figure was silhouetted in the glare of the headlights. Our blood 'froze in our veins'- – it was a policeman! He stood before us hands on his hips.

"And just where do you think you lot are going?"

A member of our party who, despite his fear, was able to speak said: "Polegate Sir."

"Polegate! Do you realise how worried your parents are? Everyone is out looking for you. Where have you been?"

Our spokesman was still able to speak.

"Eastbourne Sir, watching the men sail their boats on the pond."

"Eastbourne! You lot, hop in the back!"

He led the way and opened the rear door of the 'Wolsley' police car and we squashed ourselves onto the rear seat and the floor. We had not been arrested and we were on our way home! Arriving in Polegate the police-car stopped at each house to discharge each weary occupant into the arms of tearful but thankful mothers – and no doubt irate fathers!

I was sitting in a hot bath with my mother standing by the bathroom door with a very stern face. Our burly saviour was crouched on the floor beside me telling me what a naughty boy I had been and saying that I must promise never, ever, to do such a thing again. If I did, he would come and 'lock me up'. I sat there in the hot water, tearfully promising never, ever again would I leave home without telling my mother where I was going.

At school exciting things were taking place. Every child was issued with a gas mask contained in a strong cardboard box complete with a strong shoulder cord. Each fitting was carefully conducted by uniformed visitors and we were shown how to blow hard into the mask, and at the same time partly lifting the side of the mask to expel any trapped gas. The signal for a German gas attack was to be made by Wardens using large wooden rattles- not so dissimilar to those used by football fans today – and shouting "Gas! Gas!" To us it was all very exciting and from time to time the school conducted mock alarms to ensure that we knew what to do in the event of an attack. Part of some lessons was conducted with everyone wearing their gas masks. The only way that it was possible to communicate was to stand close to each other and raise one's voice. Trying to hear our teacher, despite her proximity, was close to impossible. There was a positive outcome: whispering in class when the teacher's back was turned ceased.

It was now September and our 'swops' in the school playground consisted of cigarette cards. Each packet of cigarettes contained a single card that formed part of a collection which depicted soldiers of the Empire dressed in their various resplendent uniforms, or R.A.F. and Fleet Air Arm aeroplanes, such as the twin-engined 'Anson', the "Oxford' and the Handley Page 'Hampden'. The Fleet Air Arm was represented with pictures of the Blackburn 'Skua' and the Gloster 'Gladiator'. Various army cap badges started to appear, with 'swops' costing as much as two or three stale cakes per badge. Boys could be heard boasting that their Dad was in the 'Royal Sussex Regiment' or the 'Grenadier Guards'. Toy soldiers made from lead had always been popular: now there was added interest as the coloured uniforms gave way to khaki, with the rifles which were once held on their shoulders now being held in both hands with the bayonets pointed ominously towards an unseen enemy.

One morning, having just drunk my cup of 'Ovaltine', I joined my grandmother in the front room and was cautioned to be quiet as the Prime Minister was soon to broadcast to the nation. I sat on my grandmother's lap as she switched on our 'Pye' radio, and once again I was cautioned to be quiet. The solemn voice of the B.B.C. announcer introduced the Prime Minister, Neville

Chamberlain. At that young age I did not listen to all the words, but I well recall his final sentence. "As a result we are now at war with Germany."

My grandmother held me tightly in her arms as the tears ran down her cheeks.

"Don't cry, grandma, I'll look after you."

With these words she broke into sobs.

I ran down the road to Peter's house full of excitement and met him in his front garden! "Peter, we're going to fight the Germans!" The words had hardly left my mouth when the air raid siren sounded! I knew what to do. I ran back home again and joined grandmother underneath the kitchen table. What would happen? Within minutes the "All Clear" siren sounded and we crawled out from underneath our refuge. It was later reported that the alarm had been sounded due to a civilian aircraft making its way to land at Croydon aerodrome.

With the onset of autumn, once again it was time to follow the local hunt that gathered at the large public house situated on the Eastbourne/Lewes and Polegate cross-roads. There was an atmosphere of mounting excitement as horses were unloaded from various large vans, their shining coats steaming in the crisp early morning air. Their riders were dressed in sporting pink (red) jackets, black velvet hats, white jodhpurs and gleaming, long leather boots. They gathered in small groups as they waited to mount their horses, their breath clearly visible as it came into contact with the crisp morning air. The thirty or so hounds were sniffing the ground, their tails wagging furiously as they sensed the expectation of the forthcoming chase. They were controlled by three grooms who, unlike the riders, wore tweed jackets and green waistcoats, their lower legs being encased in long brown leather gaiters. On their feet they wore stout, brown leather boots. At this juncture the riders mounted their horses, causing some of the hounds to start baying, as their grooms attempted to contain their growing level of excitement. Suddenly the pub's landlord appeared with a large tray of tulip-shaped glasses, filled with a yellow-looking liquid. These were handed up to the mounted riders and quickly quaffed. One of them gave a 'toot' on a small copper horn and the hunt moved slowly off, with the hounds bringing up the rear. Peter and I followed on foot until the horses broke into a canter, with the hounds now running ahead and baying with excitement. Within minutes the hunt disappeared from view, leaving Peter and I to retrace our steps to Polegate.

Little did I realise that my life was about to change! It was decided by my mother that due to the war, we should return to Brighton where the main body of our family lived.

2. "You have to be brave."

My family had originated in Brighton. My mother had been born there, had been married in St. Peter's Church when only twenty years of age, and had separated from her husband soon after I was born. Her family rallied around her and, as Victorian families were normally large, I had numerous Aunts and Uncles within the town. There were two maiden Aunts, Hilda and Rhoda; Uncle Bob, who was married to Auntie Ivy, and Uncle Bill, who was married to Auntie Lucy. I also had an Uncle Tom and Aunt Kit who resided in Polegate and who were no doubt our reason for moving there prior to the war.

As a child I had always liked Brighton. There were two piers to visit; donkey rides along the beach and trips out to sea in one of the larger fishing boats. During the summer months white, open, double- decker buses ran along the sea-front. Also during the summer the policemen wore white helmets and pale blue shirts. There were huge beds of flowers that were floodlit at night and fountains cascading water that constantly changed colour from red to yellow, then green to blue. Then there was the proximity of the South Downs and train rides to a large, natural feature called 'Devils Dyke'.

With our return to Brighton things had changed. Auntie Hilda, despite being over age, had joined the women's section of the army (known as the A.T.S.). Uncle Bob had joined the R.A.F. and Uncle Bill, who had served in the Navy during the First World War, had been drafted into the Army. Despite being a 'crack-shot' with the local small-bore rifle club, he was selected to be trained as a cook! The only impact on me was, as we now resided in Stanmer Villas and due to its proximity, I was sent to Ditchling Road School.

Within Brighton massive changes had taken place. Barbed wire now stretched along the whole length of the sea-front. There were anti-aircraft gun emplacements and the two piers had been blown in half to prevent a German invasion fleet from using them to unload troops and cargo. The 'Hollingbury Golf Course' was criss-crossed with wires supported by steel poles to prevent any landings by German gliders bearing troops. Every house window was taped to restrict flying glass caused by bombs and every window was 'blacked out' by thick, heavy curtains. Every night Wardens prowled the streets to ensure that not even one chink of light was showing.

At our school underground air-raid shelters had been dug in the playground and numerous drills were held to ensure that we vacated our classrooms in an orderly manner. Once seated inside the shelter, each teacher checked off our names against the class register to make sure that we were all there.

At first nothing happened, then one night there was an air-raid! I stood in the doorway of our house watching scores of red hot 'sticks' – which were incendiary bombs – falling to the ground and hearing the whistling of the bombs, to be quickly followed by the bright flashes at each explosion. It was all very exciting! However, I was quickly pulled indoors by my mother and we hurried to shelter under the stairs. During daylight there were numerous circling and criss-crossing vapour trails in the sky, and the chatter of machine-gun fire could be clearly heard. One day I saw a tiny figure falling from the sky, then suddenly a parachute billowed out behind it and the swaying figure below its canopy disappeared over the brow of the hill. At school boys were bringing pieces of shrapnel and spent cartridge cases. One boy brought a small piece of a shot-down German aeroplane which had been brought home by his father who was serving in the R.A.F.

Strict food rationing was in force. All tropical fruits had long since disappeared; butter was rationed to just two ounces per person per week. Cheese was a similar quantity. Meat was a meagre four ounces per person per week and it was not possible to select what you wanted – you had to take whatever was available. Fish, freshly caught off Brighton, which was once in plentiful supply, was not rationed but not always available.

At this stage we owned a dog who, due to rationing, was no doubt also feeling the loss of his usual repast. As a result he sometimes escaped and would follow the butcher's boy making his rounds by bicycle with a large wicker basket containing several families' meat rations. These were carried in a special holder situated above the front wheel. Parking the bicycle beside the front gate the boy would select the named packet and make his delivery. With an unguarded bicycle carrying parcels of raw meat, our dog would strike! It was not just the cost of having to repay the butcher for his loss, but meat was in very short supply and our dog had stolen some family's weekly ration! I was to witness our dog's thieving ways. One afternoon on my way home from school I saw our dog emerging from the butcher's shop with a string of sausages in his mouth, being hotly pursued by the butcher armed with a meat cleaver! With a pounding heart I 'shot' into the local newsagents hoping that the dog hadn't seen me. With shaking hands I had to purchase a penny HB pencil to account for my rapid appearance! Once again the butcher arrived at our front door to demand payment – and our dog's days were numbered!

One day my mother told me that I had to be very brave. The Germans could arrive any day and the authorities had decided that children should be 'evacuated' away from the danger area. She explained that this meant that I would have to go away and stay in a safe place and that she and grandma could not come with me, but I would be with all my friends from school and she would write to me very often and come to see me as soon as possible. I was to leave in a few days' time. This had come as a 'bolt out of the blue'. I didn't think it was dangerous, and what about all the 'swops' at school for bits of shrapnel and cartridge cases?

My fate was out of my mother's hands – I was to be evacuated. We were allowed only one small suitcase each which could just about hold a complete change of clothes, shoes and pyjamas. As emergency rations, parents were advised to pack two bars of chocolate into each suitcase. Chocolate! I chose my favourites. 'Fry's' chocolate bar filled with white sugar fondant and a 'Cadburys' chocolate bar filled with strawberry-coloured fondant. I was both sad and excited at the prospect of leaving my home and travelling into the unknown. However, before my departure for 'pastures new', our 'peaceful' existence was about to change!

Some weeks previously, my Aunt Hilda had arrived home unexpectedly saying that one of the officers had been rude to her and as a result she had left the army. My grandmother was horrified!

"You can't leave the army – its desertion. The police will come looking for you and you'll be arrested and imprisoned. If you were a man you'd be shot!"

Despite these protestations my Aunt was adamant – she was not going back! My Aunt wrote to the commanding officer explaining why she had left and no doubt due to her being over age she was not arrested, but was drafted into war-work, becoming an electrician's mate at the Brighton Locomotive Works. So once again with Aunt Hilda in residence we returned to normal domesticity.

There was another cause of stress and despair. My Uncle Bill had been in the pull-back through France to the beaches of Dunkirk. Having been shelled, bombed and shot at for days on end, and seeing numerous craft sunk by German air attacks, in conjunction with six of his friends they had decided to walk further down the coast in a westerly direction in the hope of finding a small boat that would get them safely back to England. Evidently the weather was idyllic and after several days without encountering any Germans, they finally arrived at a small French port to see a British destroyer blowing up harbour installations – to be informed by the crew that the evacuation at Dunkirk had finished ten days earlier! As a result, he and his comrades had been reported as 'missing in action'. Arriving in England and expecting a hero's welcome, they were met by a Regimental Sergeant Major who very quickly dispelled all thoughts of glory.

"You 'orrible lot, get fell in! Right turn. Left right, left right" – as he marched them off the quayside much to the amusement of the watching sailors.

As you can imagine, the whole family were overjoyed at his return, and in particular Aunt Lucy. I digress.

The morning for my departure arrived. Accompanied by my mother we made our way to school to find the playground packed with anxious looking parents and children clutching their small suitcases, with their gas-masks suspended on their shoulders by cords. Some mothers and children were in tears and being hugged. Faced with this sea of misery I found it very difficult not to cry. Teachers armed with pencils and lists were calling out names. As each child and parent stepped forward, a luggage label was secured to the child's coat lapel. It stated the child's full name, home address and school. Looking around I was glad to see that the girl I had a 'crush on' was also there. Perhaps I could sit beside her!

It was time to go. Before boarding the waiting coaches, mothers hugged and smothered each departing child with their final kisses, plus many "now you be good and I'll write soon and you do the same as soon as you arrive." These final parting words often caused more tears as mothers and children hugged each other and reluctantly parted, and once again promising to write soon. As I went to board the coach my reserve melted. As I hugged my mother and feeling her arms around me, the tears welled up in my eyes and commenced to trickle down my cheeks. Apart from my 'girlfriend', I was also very pleased to see that our favourite teachers were also coming with us! As the coaches departed for Brighton Station, some mothers ran alongside each coach waving to their child with tears pouring down their faces. Inside our coach some children clutched their small suitcases and openly sobbed. Faced with this scene of so much despair I just managed to stifle a sob and stared out of the window at the passing houses. Suddenly I realised this adventure had lost its allure and I surreptitiously wiped my eyes.

Arriving at Brighton Railway Station any thoughts of being beside my 'girlfriend' were quickly dispelled. As we exited the coach we were placed into pairs and told to hold hands. Clutching our suitcases, with our gas-masks bumping on our hips, we were led onto a platform, counted, and then placed into the waiting carriages. The station echoed to the chatter of hundreds of children bound for various (and to us unknown) destinations. There was a smell of smoke from the engines and pillars of steam rose into the morning air. The carriage doors were secured, the guard blew his whistle and waived his green flag – we were off on what would prove to be a very protracted journey. Some children crowded around the windows; others continued to sob, and others, despite being told not to, opened their suitcases and commenced to eat their emergency chocolate ration.

3.   "Me name's Nellie"

It was dark as the train drew into the blacked-out station. Peering through windows only revealed very vague outlines. One of our teachers appeared at the door of our compartment carrying a shielded torch.

"Now children we are staying near here for the night. Please leave the compartment and when on the platform, form up in twos and hold hands, then wait for us to come and collect you. Don't leave anything behind."

Leaving us to disembark, she then went to the next compartment to repeat the same message.

Standing on the platform of this small, strange and unknown station, clutching our small suitcases and gas-masks, holding hands we awaited her return. Talking in whispers the common topics of conversation were, "Where are we?" And, "it's dark and 'spooky'." Our other teachers arrived, and using their shielded torches, we were counted, and then moved off in pairs to some waiting coaches with very dim interior blue lights. The girl I was with held my hand even tighter. All we could see in the surrounding darkness were the outlines of the waiting coaches with their very dim blue 'spooky' interior lights. One by one we climbed aboard the steep steps into the dimly lit interior. Having sat down we were counted again. The driver started the engine and we drove off into the night, passing outlines of darkened houses. Some thirty minutes later the coach stopped besides a large single-storied building. Where were we, and what was this building? The series of hurried whispers confirmed that it was a hospital, and as we hadn't passed any houses for at least fifteen minutes, I realised that it must be situated deep in the countryside. Our teachers, carrying their shielded torches, reappeared.

"Now children this is where we are staying tonight. Once inside the entrance the girls are to form up in twos on the left and the boys in twos on the right. As at the railway station, make sure that nothing is left behind on the coach. Once outside – stay together."

We made for the exit and carefully stepped down the very steep steps onto the hard surface where our teacher was waiting. Having ensured that no one or item had been left on the coach, she joined us on the tarmac.

"Now, link up in pairs and follow me."

Due to the black-out precautions there was only shielded torch-light to guide us into the outer hall. Once inside, the door was closed and the electric lights were switched on and we were ushered into our respective groups and counted. A nurse appeared dressed in a starched white apron and a matching head-scarf and a mid-blue uniform. The way she wore her head-scarf reminded me of a picture that I had seen of an Egyptian mummy. She smiled and said: "Children, welcome to our hospital. We have a lovely hot meal waiting for you and glasses of milk. Now before you eat your supper, the girls are to follow your lady teacher and the boys this gentleman here. They will take you to where you will be sleeping tonight. When you have chosen your bed, leave your luggage beside it and wait for your teachers' instructions."

We followed Mr. Hercourt down a long corridor to where another nurse was waiting to show us into our ward. Once inside there was a scramble to choose a bed with shouts of "I'm having this one!" Or, "You can't have that bed it's for my friend!"

With order restored by Mr. Hercourt, we filed off to the dining room and sat down to plates of macaroni cheese, followed by rice pudding and jam. When we had finished eating, the only thing left on each plate was the maker's name!

We now returned to our 'bedroom', undressed and put on our pyjamas prior to washing and brushing our teeth. Several boys decided it was time to 'test' the beds and proceeded to jump up and down on the immaculate white cotton bed-covers. The re-appearance of Mr. Harcourt restored 'law and order' and it was "lights out". The giggles and comments soon subsided as sleep slowly but surely closed the eyes of our group of very tired boys.

The following morning, having had a substantial breakfast which included porridge, again we boarded the coaches and waived 'good-bye' to the nurses. They had been very kind and we had enjoyed our brief stay. The atmosphere within our group had changed – no longer were there tears and puffy eyes. We looked at the passing countryside and houses – it was all so different from the Sussex Downs and our home town! Hedges had been replaced by low, grey stone walls that had been built without the use of any mortar. The houses to my eyes looked grey and without colour. We passed flocks of sheep grazing in the fields – they had long grey shaggy coats – so unlike the white sheep that I had seen being herded on the South Downs. Despite the morning sunshine, this strange landscape seemed to affect us all – the excitement gave way to apathy and we stared silently out of the windows at this strange land.

In the early afternoon we arrived at a village of old, grey-looking houses, passing a small green with a church set well back off the road. Our coach then turned off the main road, entered a village and stopped besides a large, single-storied building that was situated next to a wood-yard with a crane clearly visible above the tall brick walling. We all filed out of the coach to be met by a group of ladies in uniform who spoke to us in very strange English. As they ushered us into the hall, words such as "luv" and "cum" were being used. Within the hall long, white cloth-covered tables that had been set out with mugs of milk, sandwiches and, what to me looked like very large flattened currant buns. Food!

On the opposite side of this large hall was another long table piled high with clothing and footwear. This, we were informed, had been supplied by Canada. Having eaten, we were taken to this table where several kind ladies proceeded to select for each of us one item of clothing and one item of footwear. My eyes lighted upon a long, brown three-quarter length heavy cotton jacket. It was lined with real sheepskin! The other attraction was its collar, which was also covered in dark brown sheepskin, and the front of the jacket was fastened with toggles. It was brand-new! I asked to try it on. It fitted 'like a glove' and when the lady pulled up the rounded collar, the warm sheepskin covered my ears and came almost to the top of my head! I looked at this kind, smiling lady.

"May I have this one please?"

"Of course you can luv, now let's find you a pair of shoes."

This time I was not so lucky – the only pair that fitted me were some brown rubber over-shoes. I didn't like them from the moment it was suggested that I should try them on. Had I been with my mother I would have refused to wear them, but faced with this smiling kind lady, I could not say "no." To the best of my knowledge I only ever wore them once.

We were now directed to go to the far end of the hall and to stand on the stage. The entrance door of the hall was opened and lots of middle-aged ladies entered and stood in groups looking at us. Every lady was talking in this very strange 'English'. Each of the ladies now commenced to select a child from our group. The lady who chose me wore round-rimmed, thick-lensed glasses; was well built with a kindly face and dressed in a dark blue coat and a small matching hat. She looked down at me.

"What's thar name?"

"It's Alastair Miss."

"Alastair, ee that's a posh name. Me name's Nellie. Now me and thee are gayin ter be good friends. So let's go home and have sum tea."

I was to discover later that, unlike her husband, Nellie always pronounced her "aitches." However, despite this I still found the local accent sounded very strange to my 'southern ears'. We left the hall hand-in-hand, with the lady carrying my small suitcase. My luggage consisted of my gas-mask and, clutched in my arms, my newly-acquired brown jacket and the over-shoes. Passing the wood-yard and some other grey-looking buildings, we turned right, and then proceeded to walk up a very steep hill. As we were passing a very large, multi-windowed building which was on our left, the lady noticed the direction of my gaze.

"That's t'mill theer." She remarked. "Jusst near top on't right is where we live."

We continued up the hill, turned right into a small cul-de-sac with terraced houses to our right and allotments to our left, where some chickens were running around.

"Have yer seen chickens before?" She asked.

"Yes Miss, lots of times."

"Well then yer won't be scared ter collect theer eggs. Rhode Island Reds are good layers."

At a mid-point along the terrace we stopped and the lady opened a low wooden gate and we walked down some concrete steps. Her handbag was opened and a key was produced and inserted into the door lock. As the door was opened I could feel the escaping heat on my face. We entered a tiny, well-lit lounge with a roaring coal fire in the grate. The lady closed the door. As I stood there the lady stepped forward and removed the mesh fire-guard, turned and said,

"Now yuung man, sit thee sen by't fire and I'll give yer a nice Yorkshire tea-cake and sum potted meat. Do yer have sugar in thee tea?"

"Yes please, just a tiny one."

She proceeded to remove her hat and coat and hang them onto a hook beside the door. As she turned towards me, I noted that beneath her coat she had been wearing a flower-patterned apron that was not so dissimilar to my grandmother's. She looked at me through her thick-lensed glasses.

"I'll say this, thar's well mannered. Now our Jack'll be home in about an hour and me husband soon after. I'll get thee tea."

She went through a door that led from the lounge into the kitchen and I could hear a kettle being filled and the sounds that told me food was being prepared.

As I sat staring into the fire with unseeing eyes, the enormity of my situation 'struck home'. This was my new home. When would I see my mother and family again? The people here were very kind, but they all spoke in this very strange manner. And what were 'tea-cakes' and 'potted meat'? The tears welled up into my eyes and started to trickle down my cheeks. I felt very lonely and knew that I must be a very long way from home. The tears continued to trickle down my cheeks and drip onto my grey shorts. My thoughts were disturbed as the lady arrived with a tea-pot in a knitted cover, and in her other hand a plate containing a sandwich and a large round, flat currant bun that was identical to the one I had seen, and tasted, at the village hall. She placed the tea-pot and plate onto the cloth-covered table, and then came over to where I was sitting on the floor by the fire. She bent down and took my hand.

"Now don't cry, cum and give me a cuddle."

She led me over to the table, sat down and invited me to sit on her lap, and then put her arms around me. She felt warm and smelled different to my mother and grandmother, but it was comforting to be held like this. She produced a handkerchief and wiped my eyes, then brushed my hair back from my forehead.

"Don't forget, all yer school friends are here and you'll see them in't morning.

Yer can go fur walks with our Jack, help feed t'chickens and collect theer eggs. Now you have sum tea."

I eased myself off her lap and sat in one of the vacant chairs. The lady proceeded to remove the knitted cover off the tea-pot and gave its contents a vigorous stir, replaced the cover and poured some tea into an enormous mug. As I watched the lady added the milk and a tiny spoonful of sugar. This enormous mug was then placed beside my plate.

"Alastair, you have a drink of sum good strong tea made the Yorkshire way."

I said "thank you" and again looked at this enormous mug of steaming tea. She noted my hesitation.

"Don't yer have muggs in't south?"

"No Miss."

"Well here we do – and as we're friends, me name's Nellie, so no more of this 'Miss' stuff. Now eat thee tea."

Having eaten in the village hall it was going to be a struggle. I bit into the generously sliced potted meat sandwich. The bread was fresh and crusty and the filling, which had a semi-coarse texture, tasted very good and was so unlike the paste fillings that came in small jars. The lady looked at me through her thick-lensed glasses.

"Well Alastair, how's t'sandwich?"

I swallowed my mouthful.

"It's very good Miss, thank you."

"Alastair, not 'Miss', it's Nellie. Now you eat oop and I'll go and get our Jack's tea ready."

Nellie went into the kitchen as I continued to slowly eat the sandwich. How was I going to manage this large flat currant bun? As I sat there, once again thoughts of home caused my eyes to fill with tears. Everything was so strange; the country-side; the houses; the way people spoke; even the food. I pushed my plate to one side and sat there with my tears once again trickling down my face and dripping onto my grey flannel shorts. I felt in my right pocket for my carefully ironed and folded white handkerchief as Nellie entered from the kitchen, went over to the dark wooden sideboard and, having opened a drawer, returned to the table with two knives and forks. She noticed my tears.

"Alastair cum here." Nellie patted her lap and once again I was cuddled in her arms.

"Now luv, don't you fret. I know yer musst be missing yer muther, but yer safer here away from those nasty Germans and all them bombs."

I sniffed and went to reach in my pocket for my pristine handkerchief. Nellie fumbled in her apron and produced her own, then held it to my nose.

"Now you have a good blow."

I did so as Nellie gently pinched my nostrils together several times, then folded my contribution into its centre and wiped my eyes.

"That's better, isn't it?"

"Yes thank you, Nellie."

It was so strange calling an adult by her Christian name. I looked up into her face and noted how her thick-lensed glasses magnified her eyes. She smiled and gave me a kiss on my forehead.

"Bye Alastair, I wish our Jack had your manners. Now you be brave as I get our Jack's tea ready."

Once again I slipped off her lap and sat on the floor beside the fire. Nellie had not mentioned how old Jack was. Perhaps he went to the Junior School, hence Nellie's comments about good manners. As I stared into the fire, in my mind's eye I conjured up various pictures of Jack. I also wondered what the upstairs of the house was like and would I have to share Jack's bedroom? Nellie reappeared from the kitchen and placed a large plate of bread and butter onto the table.

"Alastair, don't yer wont t'tea-cake?"

"No thank you Nellie, I'm very full with your sandwich."

Again it was so strange calling an adult by her Christian name.

"Then our Jack'll have it. Now when yer muther cums ter see you, I want her ter see a big strong lad, otherwise she'll think I've bin starving you, and we don't want that to happen do we?"

"No Nellie and I'm sorry that I couldn't eat the bun."

Nellie smiled at my description.

"Alastair yer in Yorkshire now, we don't have bunns, here we have tea-cakes."

Still smiling Nellie returned to the kitchen.

There was a sound of a key turning in the lock and the front door opened. Nellie called from the kitchen.

"Is that you Jack?"

"Aye Mumm, it's me."

Standing in the doorway was a young man, clean shaven and dressed in rough working clothes. He was, to my eyes, very tall and well built, with dark brown hair brushed straight back. I noticed that underneath his old woollen sports jacket he wore a striped shirt without a collar. His trousers were a mid brown and on his feet he was wearing black boots with pointed brass-capped toes and thick wooden soles. He had a kindly face, smiled and said "hello." Nellie came out from the kitchen.

"Jack, before yer've had a wash, this is Alastair who has cum all the way from t' South and from now on he's wun of t'family."

I stood up as Jack came over and looking down at me, shook my hand.

"Alastair, where's thar from?"

"Brighton, Sir."

Jack laughed.

"Yer don't 'ave ter call me Sir, me name's Jack."

Nellie interrupted our brief initial contact.

"Our Alastair's very well mannered so maybe you can learn a thing or two."

Jack winked at me.

"When I've 'ad me wash yer can tell us all about Brighton."

Hanging his jacket on a hook beside Nellie's coat, he went up the stairs two at a time.

Jack was so much older than I had ever imagined, but despite our age difference I knew that he would be a very good friend.

Some moments later Nellie appeared from the kitchen and stood at the foot of the stairs.

"Don't spend all day upp theer, yer eggs and ham are just about ter go ont' table, yer tea's ready fur pouring and yer Dad'll be in any minute."

I could hear movement upstairs and the sound of a toilet being flushed. Jack came downstairs as Nellie placed his meal on the table, consisting of three slices of ham and two fried eggs. Ham! I hadn't seen ham for months! And two eggs! This thought was pushed to one side as the flushing of the toilet had reminded me of the growing pressure in my bladder. I looked at Nellie.

"Nellie, please may I go to the toilet?"

"Of course yer can luv. Up t'stairs and it's the first door ont' left."

Nellie turned to Jack.

"Did yer hear that Jack, he said 'toilet' not 'lavatory'."

Jack looked at me and raised his eyes to the ceiling and gave me another wink.

Having located the toilet, it was with a feeling of relief that having washed my hands, I made my way downstairs. Nellie called from the kitchen.

"Alastair, did yer wash yer hands?"

"Yes thank you Nellie."

"Yer don't have ter keep saying "thank you" all the time, "yes" will do. Now you sit at t'table with our Jack and tell him all about Brighton and them Germans."

I sat at the table telling Jack all about the Palace Pier and the Western Pier; the white open decker buses in the summer; the trips out to sea in the fishing boats; the Sussex Downs; the Brighton Pavilion where a King once lived. Between mouthfuls of food Jack nodded his head and made the occasional exclamation like: "Alastair that sounds reet smashing!" Or, "That Palace Pier sounds ter be a big un."

He then asked me a question that I had been dreading. At school this had led to fingers being pointed and whispers of "He doesn't have a father." Even my cousin Bob, who was two years my senior, had in my presence conveyed this information to his friends, which made me feel different in a very unpleasant way. Now came the dreaded question.

"So, is yer Dad int' army?"

I now had this same unpleasant feeling.

"No, I don't have a Dad."

"'As 'e died then?"

"I don't know Jack."

Nellie interrupted from the kitchen.

"Jack, leave poor lad alone, it's been bad enuf leaving his muther behind. Are yer watching t'time? Don't forget it's yer 'Home Guard' ter neet. Alastair, has our Jack told yer he's a soldier?"

"No Nellie, not yet."

"Well, when he's got himself uppstairs and changed inter his uniform, if he's time he'll show you his gunn."

Taking another quick mouthful of tea, Jack pushed his chair back, looked at me and once again raised his eyes to the ceiling.

"Alastair, I'd best be off!"

With Jack's departure upstairs, once again I was sitting on the floor by the fire as there was the sound of a key being turned in the front door, and it opened. Standing there looking at me was a man of stocky build, some-what shorter than his son. He had a smiling, kind face and, like his son, was dressed in a similar manner except that on his head he he wore a stained, flat cloth cap, and on his feet, black steel-capped leather boots.

"So muther, what 'ave we 'ere?"

He removed his cap and started to take off his jacket. Nellie appeared from the kitchen with a plate of ham and two fried eggs. Having placed this on the table she said; .

"This is Alastair all the way from Brighton and, when yer've had a wash, he'll sit with yer and tell yer all about it."

As the man approached me I stood up. He smiled and shook my hand.

"So you're Alastair. Bye, that's a posh name. I don't know anuther living soul called Alastair. I'm pleased t'meet thee."

His English was even stranger than Nellie's or Jack's.

"What do I call you Sir?"

He called to Nellie in the kitchen.

"Ee muther, did yer 'ere that? Bye Alastair thars reet well mannered. Me name's 'Arold, not Sir"

Nellie's voice came from the kitchen.

"Harold get thee sen washed as them eggs'll be stone cold!"

Like Jack, Harold raised his eyes to the ceiling and he made for the stairs, as Jack appeared in army uniform with a funny-looking long, thin cap without a peak and worn on one side of his head. He was carrying a large rifle. I couldn't resist the question.

"Is it a real one and does it have bullets?"

Jack smiled and stopped at the foot of the stairs.

"Aye, it's real un an' here's t'bullets."

He felt into the side pocket of his trousers and produced five shiny brass bullets with pointed copper tops, held together with a black metal clip.

"Does it make a loud bang?"

"Aye, a very loud bang. Alastair, I musst be gayin or I'll be late."

With shouted "goodbyes", Jack closed the front door behind him.

Harold came down the stairs and sat at the table and gestured.

"Bye ek Alastair, yons a grand fire."

I noted that Harold had been given a very large cup and saucer, not so dissimilar in size to the mug that had been given to me. He filled the cup, added milk and two tea-spoons of sugar and gave it a vigorous stir. He then proceeded to pour the tea from the cup into the saucer. Carefully lifting the saucer to his lips he commenced to drink its contents accompanied with loud slurping noises. Putting down the saucer he gave me a wink.

"Yer can't beat a good cupp of tea."

He then proceeded to refill the saucer. I was fascinated and in my childlike innocence asked:

"Why don't you use a cup?"

Harold shrugged his shoulders.

"I've no idea lad. I've always 'ad me tea like this."

Harold now started to eat his ham and eggs, plus several slices of bread and butter, washed down with several more saucers of tea. He looked up.

"Do yer like rabbits?"

"I do, but I've never had a rabbit."

"In that case me lad, when I've 'ad me tea I'll show thee me rabbits."

My curiosity was at its height.

"Do you have very many rabbits?"

"Aye, about a duzen, an' more ont' way. They're 'Blue Beverins' an' 'ave wun sum prizes. Them's cupps ont' sideboard."

I had noted the silver cups on the sideboard but, as I had been more occupied with thoughts of home, I had not even considered reading the inscriptions. Harold pushed back his chair and gave a deep sigh of contentment.

"Muther, that were a real nice drop of 'am. I'll tek our yung friend 'ere t'see rabbits an' t'chickens."

We walked across the road and through a small gate in the low wooden fence. Harold looked down at me.

"Before we see t'rabbits, 'ow about seeing if them chickens 'ave laid sum eggs?"

I followed Harold to the small hen house and he lifted a flap on the outside wall, then motioned me to come and crouch down beside him.

"Cum 'ere lad an' see this."

I bent down and peered under the flap. There was a large brown chicken sitting on some straw with its back towards us. It clucked several times at our intrusion.

"Now she's about ter lay, so we'll not disturb 'er. Let's look next door."

He lifted the next flap and motioned for me to crouch down beside him.

"Put yer 'and in theer lad."

I could see a large brown egg resting on the straw and I gingerly picked it up. It was warm! I withdrew my hand and showed the egg to Harold. He smiled.

"Now Alastair, that's fur thee breakfast – a nice fresh egg."

I could hardly believe it – I had been given a fresh egg!

"Thank you, Harold. Are you sure that I can have it, as eggs are rationed?"

Harold looked surprised.

"Rationed! Not 'ere there not. Let's check rest of t'boxes."

One by one the wooden hatches were lifted and the eggs removed. Harold took a large coloured handkerchief from his trouser pocket, spread it on the ground and placed the five eggs, including mine, into its centre and knotted the corners together.

"Reet lad, we'll leave them eggs 'ere an' now let's look at them rabbits."

I followed Harold to a nearby similar-sized wooden shed. He lifted the metal latch and opened the door, then motioned for me to go inside. Lining each wall were cages containing mottled white and blue-grey rabbits. Their coats reminded me of piebald ponies and there was a smell of urine and hay. Harold tapped on the wire of one of the cages.

"This un's a champion."

Due to Harold's tapping, the rabbit put its twitching nose to the wire, then used its fore-paws to partly climb up the mesh. Harold bent down. From a small cardboard box, he picked up a wilting dandelion leaf and pushed it through the wire, where it was quickly eaten by the rabbit's very rapid chewing. Harold moved to another cage.

"Now this un's about ter 'ave sum babies so we'll not disturb 'er too much."

I had never, ever been so close to so many rabbits.

"Harold, do they all win prizes?"

"Nay lad and them that don't go int' pot."

I was shocked! Eating pet rabbits!

"You mean that you eat them?"

"Of course, theer's nowt wrong with a good rabbit pie or stew. Same with t'chickens. Wunce eggs stop I wring t'necks and the wife roasts 'em. Yer wait me lad, theer's nowt so tasty as a 'ome grown roasted chicken. Now lad, would thar like a job?"

Based on our current discourse I was not so sure.

"Every day when yer arrive 'ome from school, do yer think yer could collect t'eggs?"

"Yes please Harold, and thank you very much."

He patted me on the head.

"I'll say this fur thee lad, thars reet good manners. Now you pop over t'hut an' fetch them eggs an' we'll go back indoors."

I very carefully picked up the knotted handkerchief and gingerly followed Harold back to the house. I had an egg all to myself! Arriving back indoors I found Nellie in the kitchen.

"Nellie, look what I've got! Harold has given me an egg for my breakfast!"

I placed the handkerchief very carefully beside the sink and untied the knots.

"Did he now. So which wun is yours?"

."It's this one!"

And I pointed to my large brown egg.

"Well yung man, as it's yours we'd better mark it"

Nellie opened a drawer in the kitchen dresser, withdrew a pencil and marked my egg with a cross.

"Now I'll know it's yours. At home what time do yer go ter bed?"

"At seven o'clock."

Nellie looked down at me through her thick-lensed glasses.

"And do yer say yer prayers?"

"Yes Nellie."

"Reet yung Alastair, it's past yer bedtime and it's school to-morrer. Yer suitcase is uppstairs. I'll take yer t'bedroom."

I followed Nellie up the stairs and was shown into a small neat bedroom. It was decorated with pale- pink patterned wallpaper, there was a little bedside table, and from the ceiling hanging on a long twisted silk-covered flex, was a pink silk covered lamp shade, with a long, thin beaded fringe.

"Alastair, yer know where t'bathroom is. Don't forget ter wash yer face and say thar prayers. Now you get good nights sleep. It's school int' morning. Now don't yer be frightened, we're jusst down t'stairs and I'll leave t'door open."

Having changed into my pyjamas, I washed my face and brushed my teeth, then returned to the bedroom. I knelt beside the bed and closed my eyes. I thought how far I was away from home and prayed to God to keep my mother, grandmother and Aunts and Uncles safe. I climbed into bed. I felt very lonely and, as I recalled my home, the tears trickled down my cheeks and onto the pillow. Downstairs I could hear Nellie and her husband talking. From time to time I could overhear snippets of conversation. Nellie's words, although quietly spoken, were very clear.

"Poor little lad he musst be very tired."

There were more mumbles, and then I heard Harold's voice. It was indistinct but there was no mistaking his strange way of talking, and words that sounded like "reet" and "nowt" drifted up the stairs. I must have gone to sleep, as the next thing that I can remember was the daylight shining through the bedroom curtains and the smell of frying wafting up the stairs.

4.   "Thummp evacuee!"

It was a bright sunny morning. Nellie came into the bedroom smiling and opened the curtains.

"Bye Alastair, when I popped me head in last neet yer were fast asleep. Now you get washed and dressed and by t'time yer cum down, breakfast'll be ont' table. Theers a grand fire int' grate."

Having washed I put on my only set of clean clothes and went downstairs where, as Nellie had stated, the coal fire was burning brightly. Nellie called from the kitchen.

"Alastair, theer's cornflakes ont' table and milk's int' jugg. Help theeself ter bread and buttter."

Nellie appeared at the kitchen door.

"Now this egg of yours, how do yer like it?"

"Boiled please"

"Reet, eat upp, yer egg wont be long."

With my milk and cornflakes finished, Nellie appeared again with my egg and took the top off for me. I cut my bread and butter into 'fingers' and proceeded to dip them into the egg, as Nellie sat at the table watching me. My real egg was delicious!

"Int' morning, do yer have milk or tea?"

"Milk please."

Nellie reached across the cloth-covered table and poured me a large mug of milk. She glanced at the clock on the mantel-piece.

"Now don't be too long, it's nearly school time."

Having finished my breakfast, I went upstairs to keep my promise to my mother that I would brush my teeth every morning and every night. Having done this I went into my bedroom, folded my pyjamas and placed my dirty underwear, socks and shirt into my suitcase. Having done this, I put on my grey school jacket and went downstairs. Nellie looked down at me.

"Bye yuung man, yer looking smart. Do yer have a comb?"

"Yes Nellie."

"Then you pop upp them stairs and let me sort out that parting of yours."

On my return Nellie proceeded to re-comb my hair. She then stood back and looked at me again.

"That's better. Now put yer coat on and we'll be off."

Hand in hand we walked down the hill passing to our right the mill building that I had noticed the previous afternoon. At the bottom of the hill we turned right passing a small shop with a similar size Co-op shop next door. Nellie pointed to the first shop.

"That's clog shop. Our Jack get's his clogs theer, and Co-op is where I shop."

We continued along the street, and then turned left. Ahead of us, situated on a corner to our left was another small shop. Nellie pointed again.

"That's pie shop."

By this time the local children were also on their way to school and most of them, including the girls, were wearing wooden-soled clogs. The boys' clogs were in the form of boots and the girls were more like shoes. Irrespective of type, they all had small brass toe caps. As you would expect, I was receiving some strange looks, coupled with whispers and glances over their shoulders. The boys looked a tough lot and I had an unpleasant feeling in the pit of my stomach. No doubt to them, dressed in my grey flannel suit, grey pullover, matching socks and cap, plus my red and black school tie – I looked a real sissy.

We entered the playground where there were scores of children running around creating the noise that one always associates with crowded school playgrounds. Standing by the entrance was one of our teachers who beckoned us over. At the sight of her I felt safe. Nellie squeezed my hand.

"Now you runn along. I'll be here ter meet yer at dinner-time and after that yer'll know t'way."

I walked over to our teacher.

"Good mornnng Miss."

"Good morning Alastair. Wait just inside with the others and I'll come and tell you what to do."

Most members of our class had already arrived and were talking amongst themselves about where they were staying; the strange way the people spoke English and how grey and dowdy everything looked. Within our small group there was a lack of excitement. No doubt like me, despite being with kind people and Harold with his rabbits and chickens, the reality of our situation was beginning to take hold – we were here to stay, perhaps for a very long time.

Our teacher appeared.

"Now children, follow me. We are to go to the back of the school hall, and when all the local children have assembled, the Headmaster will introduce us to the school."

We dutifully followed and stood at the rear of the hall. A hand-bell sounded outside and soon scores of children, ranging from our ages to fourteen, filed into the assembly hall. Our presence had created considerable interest. There were numerous glances over shoulders and in the general hub-bub, the word "evacuees" could be clearly heard.

The Headmaster arrived and stood at the front of the hall. There was immediate silence. Some months later I was to discover why. He looked around and commenced to speak.

"Good morning boys and girls."

This was greeted with a chorus of: "Good morning Sir."

He was tall and of slim build. His dark hair, dark suit and unsmiling face radiated an expectancy of complete and utter obedience. Looking at him I was aware of an unpleasant feeling in the pit of my stomach. He now commenced to address the school. This is approximately what he said:

"Why you have been called here this morning is to greet our guests from Ditchling Road School, Brighton. They have come here with their teachers to avoid the bombs which are being dropped on their town by the Germans. It is our job to make them welcome and to feel at home in our school. They will be occupying the classroom currently used by 3a. At some stage in the future, when they leave here to return home to their mothers and fathers, we must ensure that they do so with very fond memories of our school. Now please stand for morning prayers."

With morning prayers completed, everyone filed off and we followed our teacher to classroom 3a, seating ourselves in the very old wooden desks. Our teacher addressed the class.

"Children, this will be our classroom until I tell you otherwise. The books we had back home are due here either today or tomorrow. Now the first part of the morning will be used to write home to your parents to let them know how you are. I will then collect your letters and arrange to have them posted. Before we do so, I would like everyone to tell the class about their new home."

A boy raised his hand.

"Please Miss, why do the people here talk in a funny way?"

Our teacher smiled.

"No doubt we sound just as funny to them as they do to us. All over England people speak in different ways."

Another hand went up.

"Please Miss; I can't understand what they are saying to me."

Another disarming smile.

"In a few days time I have little doubt you will be able to understand every word. Now, starting with the front row, please tell everyone about your new home."

The general story was one of being with kind, friendly people who ate some strange food. Potted meat and tea-cakes featured in nearly every story. There was one very outstanding story. A boy in our class had been billeted at the local Manor House and, according to him, the only next best thing was Buckingham Palace! This was greeted with several children saying "Cor, you lucky thing."

Our teacher now issued everyone with a pencil and a sheet of paper for our first letter from Yorkshire. Heads went down and arms were crooked across the desks. There were frowns, looks towards the ceiling and tears. As I wrote the words "Dear Mother" I had a lump in my throat and only just managed to stifle a sob. Many of the others were writing with tears streaming down their faces. Two of the girls were openly sobbing and being comforted by our teacher. Faced with this scene of despair, the tears welled up into my eyes as I ended my very brief letter, which read something like this:

> Dear Mother,
> I am in Yorkshire. The people where I am staying are very nice, but speak in a funny way. They have rabbits and chickens and I had a real egg for breakfast. The children here wear funny pointed shoes with wooden soles.

Lots of love,
Alastair.
XXXXX

There was a knock on the classroom door. Two of the school's older children appeared carrying a crate of milk.

"Please Miss; we've brought t'crate of milk."

They placed it just inside the door and quickly made their exit.

Our letters were now finished and it was break-time. Our group of 'puffy-eyed' children drank their small bottles of free milk and from memory no one went out to play. The main reason was, we didn't want the local children to see that most of us had been crying.

It was now time to meet Nellie at the school gate. As I walked through the playground there were very few smiles from the local children. We were 'oddities' who spoke in a 'posh' way and we didn't wear clogs. Nellie greeted me with a broad smile.

"Well Alastair, how was school this morning?"

"We had to write home to tell our parents how we were."

"Did yer mention 't'rabbits and t'chickens?"

"Yes I did Nellie"

"And having yer own special egg for breakfast?"

We were now passing the pie shop on the corner. Nellie pointed.

"Now yer see t'pie shop theer, I normally buy pies every Saturday. This Saturday I'll give yer t'muney and a jugg fur t'gravy, and yer can bring home the hot pies. Would yer like that?"

It all sounded very strange and I nodded my head.

"Yes Nellie."

By now we were passing the clog shop.

"Do yer fancy a pair of them clogs? They keep yer feet warm int' winter."

"I've never worn clogs before. Are they difficult to walk in?"

Nellie smiled and shook her head.

"Nay, not at all."

Our conversation continued as we made our way up the hill until we came to the cul-de-sac. As we entered the low wooden gate and descended the concrete steps to the front door, Nellie said:

"Guess what's fur thee dinner? You remember t'eggs yer collected? Yer've got wun of those fried with sum chips. Now what do yer think about that?"

The thought of yet another real egg, which back home were rationed, and to be served with chips, was not without its appeal!

"Nellie, thank you very much for making me such a nice dinner."

Nellie inserted her key and opened the door.

"Now you pop upstairs and wash yer hands and I'll get thee dinner."

As I washed and dried my hands I realised that despite missing my mother and family the people I was staying with we very kind, but they spoke in this very strange way. Some of the words I had difficulty in understanding. In particular I had great difficulty understanding Harold. Unlike Nellie he never pronounced his aitches and never said "and". It was always "an". Nellie called up the stairs.

"Alastair, dinner's ont' table!"

With a full stomach I was now on my way back to school and I wondered, without the protection of Nellie, how I would be received by the local children. Soon I was in the throng making steps towards the school gate. Despite my "hellos", which some of the children returned, in the main the atmosphere was strained. Words such as, "E's wun of them evacuees", or "sissy", from a group of boys, did nothing to still the growing unpleasant feeling in the pit of my stomach.

The next morning within the playground, our class banded together watching the games of 'tag' and 'hopscotch' taking place until the ringing of the school bell announced Assembly. As before, we stood at the rear of the hall and when prayers had finished, we filed off to classroom 3a to commence our first normal day.

During the weeks that followed, although still within our own class, we did start to integrate with the local children who were very curious about bombs, bullets and seeing overhead the aerial 'dog-fights'. I have no doubt that from time to time, we 'gilded the lily' in order to add to our level of acceptance with our peers.

Within the school there was a small group of boys who were recognised as the school 'toughs' and were to be avoided at all costs – which was not very easy when walking to and from school, plus being in the playground before morning assembly, at break-time and again twice in the afternoon. Another aspect of the village school was the reputation of the Headmaster who, according to rumour, had suffered 'shell-shock' in the First World War. This, it was stated, accounted for the brutal way he thrashed any boy who was brought before him for anything at all. We were also warned about a lady teacher who was quite sadistic. During her hand-writing lessons she was very fond of cracking her pupils across the knuckles with a small stick if, in her opinion, the hand-writing was not up to the expected standard. As these stories circulated within our class, we were very thankful that we had our own teachers and had not been integrated into the school.

As the weeks turned into months and the thoughts of home became a distant memory, I had now settled in with my new 'family'. Soon after my arrival the parcels from home containing my other clothing must have made Nellie very thankful as, with only two changes of clothes, she had washed and ironed mine every day.

I now had a routine. Each day after school and at week-ends, I collected the newly laid eggs. On Saturday mornings I went to the pie shop with a jug for the gravy, and then hurried back 'home' to ensure the pies and gravy were still hot. My other tasks were to help Harold clean out the rabbit hutches, and to accompany Nellie on her visits to the small Co-op store. Although I still missed my mother and family, the thoughts of crying as I had done initially, with hind-sight seemed to be 'namby-pamby' as, after all, boys don't cry!

Nellie's best friend lived very close to my route to school. Where I turned left then passed the pie shop, had I gone ahead for less than fifty yards, there on the left within a row of terraced houses, was where Nellie's friend lived. She was a very homely and kindly lady who had a member of my class staying with her which provided me with a friend from home to play with. The lady's husband worked in the mill as a bobbin maker. As a result, he had access to a lathe and wooden off-cuts. From these he produced beautiful multi-coloured wooden bowls and candle-sticks. For the two of us he produced a series of tops plus sticks, with the thin leather laces normally used in clogs providing the thongs to complete the whips. To anyone who has never enjoyed 'whips and tops' let me describe the equipment. The 'top' was made of wood and there were two types. The first was shaped rather like a 'mushroom' – the head of the 'mushroom' being about two-and-a-half inches in diameter and about half-an-inch thick. The 'stalk' of the 'mushroom' was about three-quarters of an inch in diameter, three inches long and pointed. Where the point made contact with the ground, a small nail was hammered in to prevent the point from wearing. The accompanying whip was about half-an-inch in diameter and twelve inches long. The clog lace was affixed to one end. The thong of the whip was now wound around the 'stalk' of the 'mushroom' which was placed on the ground point down and held in position with the knee. A quick pull on the thong set the top spinning at high speed. Before it lost momentum, the 'stalk' was lashed with the whip to keep it spinning. Some children were very expert and could make the 'top' fly up into the air to land some eight or ten feet away, where it continued spinning at high speed. The other type of 'top' was a solid wooden cylinder pointed at one end, and as per the 'mushroom' type, had a small nail driven into the pointed end. The other items he made for us were 'yo-yos'.

Arriving at school one day our teacher made an announcement that sent 'shock-waves' through the class. She announced that she and Mr. Harcourt were returning to Brighton. As a result, we would be integrated into the school. I recalled with horror the reports about the Headmaster, the sadistic English teacher and, as they were our age group, the school 'toughs'. Talking amongst ourselves we dreaded the departure of our two 'protectors'. A 'grey cloud' descended on the class.

The following week we became 'normal' pupils. In our class were (as expected) two of the 'school toughs' who, from their demeanour, made it very obvious that the boy evacuees were not welcome. The fact that as a group our knowledge of the 'three R's' was more advanced than the class we joined did nothing to enhance our popularity. Comments from this pair, such as "teacher's pet" ," know-alls" and "sissy", were common-place. Now that we were in their class avoidance was impossible. With a growing level of dread we evacuee boys wondered how long it would be before this pair picked on one of us. We were soon to find out.

One morning soon after our integration, having just finished our morning milk, the leader of this pair pushed me up against the wall and grabbed the front of my pullover. To say that I was frightened was an under-statement. He placed his face close to mine and I could see that he didn't brush his teeth.

"I'm gayin ter thump thee. Before we go 'ome for us dinners, me and thee are gayin ter 'ave a fight!"

My worst nightmare had come true! When he let go of my pullover I had to quickly go to the toilet! During the morning break the news spread – "Wun of the evacuees is gayin ter be 'duffed upp!"

Throughout the following lesson I could not concentrate as, in my minds eye, various scenes emerged. My front teeth would be knocked out. My nose broken, perhaps two black eyes! I was on the edge of trembling with fear. The lesson finished and when the teacher had left the classroom, the pair of toughs grabbed me and marched me out into the playground where a crowd had gathered to watch the 'sport'. There was no escape as we were surrounded by a ring of expectant village children. He faced me.

"Get thee jacket off."

My mouth was so dry I had difficulty in replying.

"I don't want to fight you, what have I done to you?"

His jacket was being held by his companion who was goading his friend to "duff me upp!" The next thing I knew was that I had been struck on the left cheek and I stumbled backwards to the shouts of the onlookers to: "thummp evacuee, 'duff 'im upp!" He came at me again. It was 'kill or be killed'. I went berserk and smashed my fist into his face and he fell down with blood pouring from his nose. He got up and came at me again. I smashed my fist into his face and he fell down again! There was no question of skill – I was being driven by fear! I was terrified and I realised that I was 'on my own'. The crowd of onlookers were now yelling for me to "dufff 'im upp", but I didn't want to fight – I was hitting him for reasons of survival! As he got to his feet I hit him in the stomach and, as he bent forward I hit him on the top of his head and around his face. He backed away. I had won! His friend now approached. Before he could even hit out at me I smashed my fist into his nose! He reeled back, his nose was bleeding and he started to cry. I was still trembling with fear. Were there any more? My first opponent came up to me and, from a distance, said:

"We'll 'ave anuther fight after us dinners."

The crowd parted and some of them patted me on the back as I made my way towards the playground exit. I was still shaking with fear about yet another encounter with this 'school tough' and his friend.

Arriving 'home' later than usual Nellie called from the kitchen.

"Alastair, why are yer so late? Yer dinner's spoiling."

Entering the lounge she noticed the large bruise on my left cheek.

"Alastair, have yer bin fighting?"

"Yes Nellie, but I didn't want to. Two boys in our class picked on me and they want to fight me again when I get back to school."

Nellie tut-tutted.

"Let me have a look at that bruise."

She touched it very gently and I winced with pain.

"Yer very lucky it wasn't yer eye. Do yer want me ter cum t'school with yer?"

I was dying to say "yes", but for some unknown reason I said "no."

Nellie looked at me through her thick lenses.

"Now if them boys get onto yer again, I'm gayin down t'school ter see Headmaster. Yer may be a long way from home luv, but Nellie won't have any nonsense from any of them boys. Now you wash yer hands and I'll put dinner ont' table."

Having eaten it was now time to return to school. As I opened the door to leave, Nellie called to me from the kitchen.

"Now don't you forget, if them boys get onter yer let me know and I'll sort 'em out!"

It was wonderful knowing that I could rely on Nellie for protection, but every step down the hill took me closer and closer to another fight.

As I entered the playground the word spread that I had returned. I had the same horrible feeling in the pit of my stomach and I wanted to go to the toilet. Before I could do so, my opponent approached. I noticed that his nose and cheeks were swollen and he was wearing a clean shirt. I also noticed that there had been an attempt to wash the blood off his jacket. He stopped some five feet away.

"Thee an' me won't fight agin terday." And he turned and walked away. I couldn't believe it! He didn't want to fight me!

Despite this totally unexpected reprieve I still had this horrible feeling in my stomach.

I was quickly to discover that my (unwarranted) reputation had risen 'ten-fold'. Boys who would never bother to invite me to join in their games now sought my company. I was invited to be shown how to 'tickle' trout, where to pick bilberries on the local moor and where, not far away from where I was living, there was a reservoir containing huge trout! However, I am jumping ahead.

Arriving home after school Nellie sought my assurance that "them boys" had not got onto me again. With the arrival of Jack home from work and noticing my bruised cheek, he insisted that I tell him all about the fight.

"So yer knocked 'im down and really thumped 'im good an' proper?"

He smiled and ruffled my hair.

"Bye I thawt yer 'ad the look of a boxer about yer!"

Harold arrived home to be told by Jack that I had been in a fight at school "an' 'e thummped them two class 'tuffs'."

Harold was delighted and patted me on the back and wanted to know every minute detail. Nellie called from the kitchen.

"Harold, yer not ter encourage Alastair ter fight!"

Harold gave me a wink.

"Lad only defended 'is-self. Isn't that reet Alastair?"

Rather like my school, I had also gone up 'ten points' in Jack and Harold's estimation of their evacuee from Brighton. Now, I don't know if Nellie was secretly pleased, but when I arrived home the following afternoon, I was greeted with a beaming smile.

"Alastair, yer've been such a good boy, I've bought yer a present. It's int' bag theer beside t'fireplace."

A present! I pulled the box from its brown paper bag. It was a cut-out model of a battleship – H.M.S. Hood! I was 'over the moon' – a cardboard battleship! I went over and hugged Nellie round the waist.

"Nellie, thank you so much: a battleship!"

5.   Getting it 'in the neck'

At least four weeks had passed since my arrival at my new home. Each day after school I collected the eggs, and at weekends helped Harold with his rabbits and attended church with Nellie. I hadn't fully adjusted to my new life in Yorkshire but perhaps this routine helped me to 'settle in'. The other routine was attending the village school. Each morning having finished my breakfast, I climbed the stairs to brush my teeth, and I was now ready for Nellie's pre-school inspection which normally consisted of adjusting my tie and 'sorting out' my parting. This morning was to be no exception. Nellie handed back my comb.

"Alastair, yer need a hair-cutt. I'll meet yer after yer've finished school for t'day and I'll take yer t'barbers."

My 'heart sank'. I never enjoyed visiting the hairdressers as all the clipped hairs always went down my collar. In addition, the two 'school toughs' had very short, almost cropped hair which added to their fearsome appearance. There was no escape – Nellie would be taking me to the barbers. As I set off down the hill in my mind's eye I conjured up various post barber visits. Would I look like the two 'school toughs', or like many of the boys, with what was known as 'short back and sides'?

Following my afternoon lessons, as promised, Nellie was waiting at the school entrance. She gave me a beaming smile.

"So, what did yer learn terday?"

I looked up at her.

"We did adding up and taking away, some history which was all about a very famous sailor called Sir Francis Drake, and some other things."

Nellie smiled.

"Wasn't he the wun who put down his cloak for t'Queen to walk on?"

"Yes" I added "and it covered a puddle."

Nellie's next words brought me back to reality.

"Reet, let's be off t'barbers."

The barber's was near the 'Co-op' and proclaimed its 'presence' by a long pole decorated with red and white painted stripes that wound their way down its length. It had a small window which displayed some very faded advertisements for razor blades and shaving brushes. The shop's appearance did nothing to ease the growing unpleasant feeling in my stomach. As we entered, a little bell attached to the rear of the door 'tinkled', causing the barber to briefly stop applying the clippers to an old man's neck.

"I've almost finished tak a seat."

He inclined his head at four old wooden chairs and continued to apply the clippers. There were two things I noticed immediately. The place was 'scruffy' and the current client would be leaving with most of his hair on the floor! Having finished the job, the barber flicked the back of the man's neck with a small brush and, with a flourish, removed the cloth that had been covering his client's shoulders. The man stood up and looked into the mirror positioned in front of the chair.

"Bye, that looks better!"

If this is what he thought, then he was easily pleased! During this episode my eyes had been attracted to a partly stained card headed in capital letters 'PRICE LIST'. This was followed in smaller print by just two lines:

Notching: tuppence.

Haircut: sixpence.

As the customer paid for his 'haircut' I noticed that the barber had a limp. Coupled with his short stature, his short grey hair and round steel-rimmed glasses; to my eyes it gave him a sinister appearance. He turned to Nellie.

"It's short back an' sides then?"

Using a broom he swept the previous customer's silver-grey hairs into a corner, then turned to me and indicated the chair. I sat down with a rising feeling of dread. He placed the cloth around my shoulders and tucked it non to gently, into my collar. I looked at my unsmiling face in the mirror. He turned to Nellie.

" 'Ow nucch off t'top?"

Nellie's words did nothing to reassure me.

"Not too mucch, just make him look smart."

To my ears these words were 'poetic licence!

He stood behind me and looked at my reflection in the mirror.

"So yer don't want it notched' then?"

As I didn't understand the term I shrugged my shoulders. He continued.

"Sum lads 'ave it notched."

I remained silent. He reached into the top pocket of his mid-brown overall and produced a comb, then proceeded to re-align my parting, and as the comb 'dug in', causing me to sink my head into my shoulders. He reached forward to the small wooden table to the front of my chair and picked up a large pair of scissors. He turned to Nellie.

"Not too mucch off t'top?"

Without further 'ado' he proceeded to lift my hair with the comb and remove lengths of it from the top of my head. I stared into the mirror, watching in horror at the amount of hair falling onto my shoulders and the dark brown linoleum floor. Within minutes I was starting to resemble my idea of a convict! Worse was to follow! He reached into his pocket, produced a handkerchief and blew his nose very loudly, then leaned forward and placed the scissors onto the table and picked up the clippers. He stood behind me again and looked at my reflection.

"Yer've got very thick 'air, 'as anywun ever told yer that?"

I simply shrugged my shoulders. He turned to Nellie.

"Lad dusn't say mucch."

Nellie retorted,

"He dus normally."

The barber tugged the hair on the back of my head.

"Yer need sum off 'ere."

With these words he squeezed the clippers close to my left ear and 'went to work'! The clippers were applied with vigour and dug into my scalp removing almost every vestige of hair and leaving a trail of exposed skin in their wake. I made a sharp intake of breath and slightly ducked my head. The response was immediate.

"Don't wriggle around! He looked again at my reflection in the stained mirror.

"Yer anuther lad who dusn't like clippers."

Some minutes later he arrived by my right ear and, having left the usual trail of skin, again stood back to admire his 'work'. He had finished! I was wrong!

"Yer needs a bit more off."

Again the comb and scissors were applied to the sides and the top of my head. Looking into the mirror I felt that I should leave wearing my jacket over my head! Nellie paid and we went out into the daylight.

"So how wus that then?"

I had to say it.

"I look dreadful and the clippers hurt my neck."

Nellie 'tut-tutted.

"I think yer look very smart!"

Smart! Tomorrow I would have to face my Brighton class-mates looking like an escaped convict!

Soon all the boys from Brighton would 'suffer' at the hands of 'the demon barber'. As a result our overall appearance blended in with the village boys. The only two 'hairstyles' available were 'short back and sides' and 'notching', which cost only tuppence. I was to discover that 'notching' was achieved by placing a pudding basin onto the head. Any hair showing beneath its rim was soon reduced to skin length by vigorous application of the hand-held clippers. With the basin removed any hair remaining on top of the head was cut very short with scissors. The total 'operation' was completed within minutes, hence the lower price. Evidently two sizes of pudding basin were used. A medium 'two pounder' for the boys and a larger one for the men. Harold and Jack preferred 'short back and sides'.

As far as the girls were concerned they never looked any different. Perhaps their hair was treated in a much more 'genteel' fashion.

As the weeks turned into months we integrated more and more with the village children. Initially we still had separate lessons conducted by our own teachers; as a result our integration was sporadic. When our teacher finally departed our integration became complete. About this time stories about the human body started to circulate within our 'ranks'. On this subject I can only speak on behalf of the boys. Before the reader wishes to ensure that young eyes will not be allowed to read this section, please be assured that what follows, is confined to one specific area – the neck. This first came to my notice when I observed one of the village boys was noted to have his head inclined to one side. A few days later another village boy was observed with his head in a similar position. On closer inspection, both boys had pink adhesive plasters attached to the back of the neck and positioned just about level with the top of their shirt collars, the plasters being attached to the same side as the inclination. So what was the cause of this strange behaviour? In a word boils. This was something that we Brighton boys had never experienced. We were to discover that the sufferers were divided into three 'camps', each one having its fervent supporters as to how to deal with, and cure, boils. These were: The 'squeezers', the 'hot bottlers' and the 'slashers'. In every instance we were informed that it was important that the boil was 'ripe'. If at this stage you are feeling 'squeamish', be warned, worse is to follow! There was one common factor with all three 'cures', the pink sticking plaster was essential. The 'squeezers' method I leave to the reader's vivid imagination. We now come to the 'hot bottlers'. For this a beer or lemonade bottle was partly heated in the oven, then filled with very hot water, left for a short period and drained. The open neck was applied to the boil. The supporters of this method assured us, '"As bottle cools it draws t'puss out." Ugh! The 'slashers' had their mothers lance the boil with a razor blade! I will not mention the end result. I must admit that the thought of developing boils caused me some concern. Boils were obviously very painful. As one boy told us, "They 'urt like 'ell!" And I have no doubt each 'cure' was equally painful.

So what was the cause of boils? A poor diet? Poor hygiene? All I can say is that throughout my sojourn in Yorkshire I never developed this painful condition, nor can I recall any of the boys from Brighton suffering a similar fate. However, there was one thing we boys could not avoid – visiting the village barber! My initial visit was the first and only time that I was accompanied by Nellie. I hated going knowing full well not only the end result, but the application of the hand-held clippers that were always dug into my neck – and the 'scruffy' appearance of the shop's interior. From memory, I cannot recall the advertising material or the decor and fittings ever being changed.

6. Rabbits with winning ways

I was helping Harold clean out the rabbit cages and putting in fresh hay and sawdust. Hay. It always had a sweet smell and always reminded me of the warm days of summer. As a result I would often pull a handful from the storage sack and hold it to my nose, breathing in its scent. I had just returned into the hut having dumped a shovel of soiled straw and sawdust onto the compost heap. Harold, who was tending his rabbits turned and looked at me. He had a warm smile on his face.

"Alastair, dus thar like rabbits?"

"Yes Harold and this one is my favourite."

I tapped the mesh on the cage of one of the newly 'arrived' rabbits which was now about six months old.

"Yer've chosen well lad, it's a good un. 'Ow would yer like ter cum with me ter Bradford ter't rabbit show? We'll tek yer favourite an' t"champion?"

A rabbit show – at a place called Bradford. It sounded exciting!

"Harold, yes please! When is it?"

Harold ruffled my hair and gave me a knowing wink.

" Yer wont 'ave ter wait long, it's next week-end. We'll travel theer ont buss and then in Bradford, we'll tek tram ter t'top of 'ill ter t'show. Muther will make sum sandwiches, so we won't starve."

I was very excited! I had never been to a rabbit show and I hadn't been on a bus for ages. I gently tugged at Harold's sleeve.

"Harold, what do I have to do?"

He looked down at me still smiling.

"Look after t'rabbits. Now let me show yer what them judges look fur."

He took 'the champion' out of its cage and having cradled it in his arms, gently blew on the patch of grey fur on its side.

"Cum 'ere an' see this."

Harold continued to blow on the rabbit's patch of grey fur.

"Do yer see all them circles int' fur? Judges look fer perfect culours, pluss t'size of t'rabbit. It mussn't be fat or thin, butt just reet. Now let's see thee favourite. Go on, you get 'im."

I turned the wooden catch on the cage door, reached inside and carefully picked up 'my' favourite rabbit. The reason why this one was my favourite was, it always came when I tapped the wire on the front of the cage and never struggled when it was removed for cleaning. Harold stood beside me.

"Reet, you blow on't fur an' tell me what yer can see."

I blew on the same place as Harold had done and saw a series of concentric circles of varying shades of grey. Harold posed a question.

"Well, 'ow does them culours compare wit t'champion? Better, or about t' same?"

I stood there with the rabbit cradled and docile in my arms. I looked thoughtful as I considered Harold's very important question.

"I would say a little better."

Harold nodded.

"But 'ow is it better? That's a question t'judges will ask."

I looked at 'my' rabbit's fur then looked at Harold.

"I think the colours look richer than and not as pale as the other rabbit."

Harold ruffled my hair again and grinned.

"Bye ek Alastair, yer've a good eye fur 'Blue Beverins'."

Arriving back at the house, as usual, I found Nellie in the kitchen.

"Nellie, Harold is taking me to the rabbit show at a place called Bradford, and we will be going on a bus!"

Nellie looked down at me.

"Did he now? In that case yer'll need sumthing ter eat."

As the week progressed my excitement mounted. On the day of our departure, Harold took me over to the rabbit shed where two small rabbit boxes with leather carrying straps were stacked in the centre of the floor. Harold tapped the side of his nose.

"I'll tell yer me secret, but don't tell anywun else. It's important that t'rabbits arrive both looking good an' feeling good. So plenty of warm 'ay an' a carrot ter nibble on. When carrying t'box on t'buss, don't thummp t'box around. This way, theer all reet an' ready fur t'judges."

With the 'champion' and 'my' favourite now safe and sound in their carrying boxes, and having said good-bye to Nellie, Harold and I set off down the hill. In our jacket pockets we had a packet of sandwiches, which Nellie had carefully wrapped in a layer of paper. I sensed that Harold was in a jubilant mood. On each shoulder, supported by their straps, were the two rabbit boxes. As we proceeded towards the village, from time to time I attempted to steady the gently swaying boxes, and trying not to hinder Harold's progress. At the bottom of the hill we turned left, passing the village hall where I had first met Nellie, then down the street to the bus stop which was on the main road. Harold carefully placed the boxes onto the ground, then stood up and rubbed each shoulder, grinning as he did so. It was obvious that Harold was feeling very pleased with himself.

"Bye Alastair, them boxes aren't 'eavy, just awkward like ter carry . Now wot would yer say if I told thee we could win top prize terday?"

A top prize!

"Do you really think so Harold?"

He looked down at me and tapped the side of his nose.

"Aye I do lad, I do. But yer haven't asked me which wun will win t'prize. So you tell me."

The thought of 'my' favourite rabbit winning a top prize was beyond my wildest dreams!

"I hope that it will be mine. Am I right Harold?"

"Your t'judge me lad, so I'm not saying. Eh upp, 'ere cums t'bus!"

Having boarded the bus and placed the two rabbit boxes underneath the stair-well, we sat on the long seat just inside where Harold could keep his eyes on his rabbits. The lady ticket-collector pressed the bell twice, the bus gave a small lurch and we were off! From memory, when Harold paid for our fares the lady ticket collector stated that we would have to change buses at least twice before we arrived in Bradford. I hadn't been on a bus for ages, and when I was with my mother, due to my insistence we always travelled on the top-deck. My favourite seat was in the front, from where I could see all the cars, vans and people below us on the pavements and the numerous shops. However, we had to guard the rabbits and as the seats opposite were unoccupied, I was able to see the passing countryside.

When we arrived in Bradford it was a dull, overcast day. The town was larger than I had imagined. There were numerous grey buildings; the people dressed mainly in dark drab clothing and a few were wearing clogs. To my eyes Bradford matched the weather. Harold obviously knew the way. Being careful not to bump the boxes, we made our way to a tram stop. The trams were so noisy compared to the buses. They 'clanked' and 'whirred', their metal wheels adding to the noise as the wheels ran on metal rails partly buried in the road. I had never seen a tram before and I was amazed to see that protruding from its upper-deck were two long arms that connected to twin over-head wires that followed parallel to each side of the road. The front and rear of the trams, unlike the busses, were round-ended. Harold explained.

"Do yer see them long arms ont' top of t'tram? Well, when they get ter end of t'journey, driver 'ops out an' uses a greatt big pole ter un'ook 'em an' 'e puts 'em tuther way round. Now what do yer think of that?"

I could hear the noise of our approaching tram; it was time to pick up the two boxes. Having boarded, as it set off up the hill it was even noisier than I had imagined. It 'clanked' and 'whirred', the steel wheels in the rails rumbled beneath our feet. Com-pared, buses were 'havens of peace'. At the top of the hill the tram stopped. Harold carefully picked up the two boxes and we stepped down onto the road. As the tram noisily departed, I wondered how the rabbits must have felt at the totally unex-pected level of noise. Harold hitched the two carrying straps onto his shoulders. We crossed the road and made our way to a large hall. Having entered, it was obvious that Harold was well known as he was greeting, and being greeted by, dozens of people with comments such as: "'Ave thee got a couple of good uns theer?" Or. "I thowt thar'd eaten them two be now!"

The hall was packed with men and rabbits. Harold tapped me on the shoulder.

"Alastair, theers more rabbits in this 'all than thar can 'shake a stick at'."

We went to our allotted position and Harold carefully placed the boxes onto the trestle table. He bent down and whispered:

"Another of me secrets is ter let t'rabbits settle down after t'journey. We've bags of time ter brush 'em upp before t'judging starts. Now you wait "ere an' I'll go an' see wots wot."

When Harold returned I gathered from his breath that "wots wot" must have included a glass of beer!

It was announced over the loudspeaker that the initial judging would commence in thirty minutes time. Harold now carefully removed our two rabbits from their boxes and placed them into the cages that had been provided, and then placed the travelling boxes underneath the trestle table. At the far end of the hall I could see three men in long, white overall-type coats who were looking closely at each rabbit, as their proud owners stood back in the gangway. I could see one of the men was writing on a clip-board, which was about the size of a sheet of foolscap paper. We continued to wait and my initial excitement was starting to wane.

"Harold, will it take a long time before the prizes are announced?"

"Aye lad, what them judges are doing now is ter sort out 't'sheep from t'goats'. If they don't stop 'ere fur more than a few minutes, we might just as well go 'ome. Judging will go on well inter t'afternoon. It can't be russhed. You go on over theer an' see wot them judges are upp to."

I wandered around the hall. There were all sorts of rabbits and it was then that I realised that there were several classes to be judged – hence Harold's comment that "It would be well into the afternoon before our results would be announced." The most striking rabbits on display were white with very long, soft fur. Pervading this whole show was the smell of urine and sawdust – a smell that was now very, very familiar to my nostrils.

I walked over to stand as close as I dare to the three judges to observe exactly what they were doing. I noted that not every rabbit was removed from its cage. Those that were inspected from various angles; were felt all over; had their ears gently stroked; their eyes looked at and some had their fur blown on. One of the judges was using his fore-finger to stroke the rabbit's fur 'against the grain'. The judges then all conferred, made notes and sometimes glanced again at the number of the display cage, then moved on. I returned to report to Harold.

About mid-day the judges arrived at our section. As I had observed previously some rabbits were examined more minutely than others. They now stopped to view our two rabbits! I was on tenter-hooks! Would they stay more than a few minutes? They examined 'the champion' from the outside of his cage. Now one of them reached inside and picked the rabbit up. The other two judges stepped forward and the rabbit was examined with extreme care – and then I saw one of them blow on its grey fur! So Harold hadn't been telling me 'whoppers'. The 'champion' was examined from every angle; felt all over and even had its teeth examined! As the judges conferred I tried to hear what was being said. Due to the overall noise within the hall I couldn't hear a word. The rabbit was returned to its cage and its number noted. Now it was 'my' rabbit's turn. As with 'the champion' it was examined all over; blown on; teeth examined and had its eyes checked. Heads went together, notes were made and they moved on. I gently tugged at Harold's coat sleeve and said in a soft voice, "They stayed a long time; do you think we'll get a prize?" Harold tapped the side of his nose and closed one eye in an extended wink.

"I think we're in with a good chance."

Some thirty minutes later the judges returned and spoke to several of the men in our section, including Harold. I could tell by the expression on Harold's face that it was good news! He came over with a broad grin on his face.

"Guess wot? We're int' final! You wait 'ere and I'll jusst go an' see them initial results ont' board over theer."

Harold was away for ages, but I dare not leave the rabbits – we were in the final! When Harold returned it was again obvious by his breath that checking the initial results had included another glass or beer! In his hands he was carrying a bottle of 'Dandelion & Burdock', which was a soft, fizzy drink and looked like the colour of very weak tea. In his other hand was a packet of 'Smiths' crisps, which included a very tiny twist of blue paper containing salt.

These two items were handed to me as if it was the actual prize giving.

"'Ere lad, get stuckk inter these!"

The bottle of 'Dandelion & Burdock' was something that I had never experienced in the South of England, but having been in Yorkshire for some time I had now acquired a taste for this 'Northern' brew. Having had nothing to drink since leaving 'home', I twisted open the black stopper with its orange rubber seal, put the bottle to my lips and had a long drink. Nectar! I was just about to take another drink when Harold said,

"Aye upp, t'judges are cuming back, put t'bottle an' crisps under t' table."

This time the examination of the 'Blue Beverins' in the final seemed to take ages and ages. There was much note taking and lots of head nods. I could feel my level of excitement mounting! Would we win a prize? Another thirty minutes or so later the names of the winners of each rabbit class were announced.

Now it was our class. I could hardly breathe as the announcement commenced:

"In the Blue Beverin' class the first prize goes to number two sixty one."

The 'champion' had won! The announcement continued.

"And the runner up is......"

'My' rabbit had come second! Two winners! I was 'over the moon'! Harold went forward to receive the two prizes and, I suspected, a sum of money. He returned to the stand beaming from ear to ear!

"Alastair, ont' way 'ome, me an' thee is gayin ter 'ave a drink!"

We left the hall with our two winners safely ensconced in their travelling boxes and made for the tram stop. Having boarded the tram, as before the two boxes were placed carefully underneath the stair-well and we sat on the long side seat just inside. The tram whirred and rattled its way down the hill, accompanied by the rumbling of the steel wheels on the tram-lines. Almost opposite to where we had originally boarded the other tram, it stopped. We alighted and Harold looked around. On a nearby corner there was a public-house. Harold was in an expansive mood.

"Now Alastair, at t'pubb you sit ont' boxes by t'door ter guard t'rabbits. Yer can 'ave anything, anything at all."

He waived his right arm across his chest like some benevolent philanthropist.

"Can I have a glass of still lemonade and a packet of crisps please?"

"I'll do better than that lad, 'ow about a pie?"

Before I had time to consider Harold's suggestion, he placed the two carrying straps onto his shoulders and we crossed the road.

Arriving outside the public-house, Harold placed the two boxes beside the doorway and entered the swing doors. I could smell cigarette smoke and beer. As instructed, I sat on the boxes guarding the rabbits. About five minutes later Harold returned and handed me a pint glass of still lemonade, a packet of crisps and a warm brown-looking pie.

"Pie's meat an' tatties. I wont be long."

I sat on the rabbit boxes and between large sips of lemonade I commenced to eat my food. The pie tasted good but if there was meat in it, they must have overlooked mine. The light started to fade. Having drunk a pint of lemonade I was conscious that I needed to go to the toilet. Harold was still inside the public-house and I was becoming more desperate by the minute! At long last Harold reappeared and I noticed that he seemed to be having some difficulty with his feet.

"Harold, I need to go to the toilet, I'm desperate!"

"Yer can't go inter t'pub. Go round t'corner theer an' 'ave a widdle against t'wall."

I was shocked!

"I can't do that! What if someone sees me?"

"No wun's gayin ter mind a little lad like thee. Go an' 'ave thee widdle and we'll catch t'buss fur 'ome."

Being desperate, but highly embarrassed, it was with a feeling of extreme relief that I returned from round the corner and in the surrounding gloom of the 'black-out' we headed for the bus-stop. From time to time throughout the journey, Harold closed his eyes, his head dropped lower and lower and he started to snore. At this he woke up, grunted, then minutes later his head dropped down again. I was becoming concerned, as we had to change buses. By constantly tugging at Harold's sleeve, more by good luck than judgement we made the correct changes.

By the time we arrived in the village it was dark. There was not a glimmer of light anywhere. As we crossed the road opposite the church, passing the village hall and the saw-mill, my eyes had adjusted to the surrounding darkness. We turned right and commenced walking up the hill, passing the now darkened and silent mill, its huge bulk standing out against the night sky. Due to the 'black-out' and lack of any traffic, we walked in the centre of the road, which was a bonus as Harold, who was carrying the rabbit boxes, was finding it difficult to walk in a straight line. As we continued up the hill, I also noticed that Harold was still having trouble with his feet, as from time to time he would stumble. Since leaving the bus, every few minutes Harold started to sing in a soft voice, talk to himself about the rabbits, then try to hug me, saying I was a champion boxer and what a grand lad I was.

We now arrived at our front door and Harold felt in his various pockets, paused, then talking to himself he repeated the same performance several times. The door opened! From the expression on her face it was obvious that Nellie was very annoyed!

"Why have yer kept this boy out until this time of neet? Cum in here, yer drunk!"

With the door closed behind us Harold stood there beaming at Nellie and had difficulty standing still.

"Cum 'ere an' give us a kiss."

He took two unsteady paces towards Nellie who pushed him away.

"Go away yer daft 'aparth' and get ter bed!"

Harold stood there still unsteady on his feet and with a stupid grin on his face.

"We wun Nellie, we wun! An' Alastair 'ere guarded t'rabbits all day. Bye yer a grand lad."

He put his arm around my shoulder and gave me a hug. Nellie was not impressed!

"It's way past Alastair's bed time, yer ought ter be ashamed of yerself!"

She turned and faced me.

"Now, I know what he's had, but what have you had ter eat all day?"

"I've had your sandwiches, some lemonade, crisps and a pie."

With these words Harold fumbled in his jacket pocket and with a beaming smile produced his packet of rather squashed sandwiches. He stood there with the same stupid smile and held out the packet to Nellie.

" I didn't 'ave time ter eat 'em."

I could see that Nellie was furious!

"It's justt as well, that's all that thar'll get fur thee supper! Alastair go upp stairs and put yer pyjamas on and then cum down again."

As I walked up the stairs I realised that our joint win had not been well received and Harold was 'in the dog box'.

Having washed and changed I went to go downstairs. Harold was there on the landing dressed only in his long-tailed shirt and making his unsteady way towards the bathroom. He paused and stood there with the same stupid grin on his face, holding onto the wall for support. With difficulty and several misses, he tapped the side of his nose.

"Alastair, we wun! Bye yer a reet grand lad."

Nellie's voice came up the stairs.

"Harold, leave Alastair alone and git ter bed! Alastair yer suppper's ont' table."

I cannot recall what the meal was, but it was hot and satisfying. Before I had finished eating, loud snores could be heard coming from upstairs. Some moments later Nellie appeared holding Harold's trousers. She commenced to empty the pockets. Noting my expression she looked at me.

"All I'm doing, Alastair, is rescuing next week's housekeeping muney."

In the weeks and months that followed I was to learn that Harold normally came home drunk on pay day and that he always slept in the shirt he wore to work. Following each pay day, as Harold lay snoring in his bed; Nellie would bring his trousers downstairs and remove from the pockets next week's housekeeping money. Even at my early age I realised that Harold's drunken state on pay day was wrong, but he was never violent and had a 'heart of gold'. Despite the fact that I had never, ever seen anyone drunk before, I was not shocked and never had cause to be frightened.

7. "He sings like an angel."

With the passage of time I had settled in to my new environment. With my fight in the school playground almost a distant memory, plus being accepted by the local boys of my own age group, life was pleasant. I still collected the eggs each day, helped feed the chickens and assisted Harold to look after the rabbits. Nellie always provided good and plentiful food, which was sometimes supplemented with one of Harold's roasted chickens, and from time to time I went for countryside walks with Jack and his girlfriend. What more could a boy want? Human nature being what it is, when people are happy they sing, and I was no exception.

Within a few weeks of my arrival, Nellie had ascertained that I was 'Church of England'. As a result, I now attended Sunday school and received an attendance booklet into which I dutifully stuck one stamp per attendance. The stamps depicted various religious scenes and, with the passage of years, I cannot recall if there was a prize for having a full book. This led to accompanying Nellie to church on Sunday mornings, leaving Harold to attend to his chickens and rabbits.

To return to my singing. Nellie was in the kitchen as I gave tongue to a song that my Aunt Hilda had taught me several years previously. It was 'Red Sails in The Sunset'. The lyrics were very sentimental and the song was about a girl waiting for her fisherman boyfriend. "Red sails in the sunset, way out on the sea; red sails in the sunset bring him safely to me."

Nellie's head appeared round the kitchen door.

"Alastair, yer should be int' church choir. Do yer fancy that?"

As I was not overly fond of Sunday school and sitting on a hard pew with Nellie listening to the Vicar's long sermons, I was not sure if I wished to add another layer onto my ultimate route to salvation.

"I don't know Nellie."

If Nellie detected a negative tone in my response she ignored it.

"If yer like, I'll talk ter t'vicar after church next Sunnday."

My fate was sealed. Little did I realise that my burst into song would take me into another world, a world where many pleasures lay in store for a small boy who was a long way from home.

Sunday morning arrived and, dressed in my 'Sunday best', with Nellie dressed in a navy-blue top coat and a matching hat with a narrow brim, we set off down the hill to church. On the way we encountered other lady church-goers and I was introduced as, "This is Alastair, my little evacuee."

All the ladies were around Nellie's age and, being a village, on route much gossip was exchanged about sons who were away in the forces; how small the war-time rations were and general female 'chit-chat'. Anything that my young ears should not hear, was done in whispers or something that I came to know as 'lip-reading,' which was used by the women mill-workers as the noise of the machinery made normal speech impossible. It was obviously effective as I never 'heard' a thing.

Having entered the church, Nellie curtsied at the altar, and then gently squeezed my hand and I was led to a pew very close to the front of the church in order that I could observe the choir. We sat right next to the aisle. Nellie knelt briefly in prayer, then sat back and looked at me through her thick glasses. She leaned towards me and whispered,

"From here yer can see all the choir-boys, where they sit and what they have ter do."

With these words the organist commenced to play and the congregation stood as, headed by a senior member of the choir carrying a large brass cross on a long polished wooden pole, followed by the Vicar with his head partly bowed and looking very solemn, they walked ahead of the senior members of the choir who, as they filed past, also had the same solemn expression. Dressed in their long black cassocks and three-quarter length white surplices, their hair 'plastered down' with a wet comb, the choir-boys looked angelic. I recognised some of them, as five were in my class at school. Reaching the two steps that led to the altar, the procession paused, and then bowed their heads towards the altar. The choir, led by the boys, filed off into the choir-stalls, the boys sitting in the front rows. The Vicar knelt before the altar in prayer, then stood and faced the congregation.

"We will commence with the hymn 'Fight the Good Fight with all Your Might!".

As we were at war, this choice was always popular and was rendered with gusto!

Throughout the service, some of the choir-boys still looking angelic and with solemn faces, assisted the Vicar at the altar. Little did he realise that despite their angelic appearance his choir-boys included a large percentage of miscreants who were not averse to stealing apples from peoples' gardens, (known in the village as 'scrumping'), plus various other illegal acts that had yet to come to the attention of the village policeman. Now two of them were standing as close to the altar as the Vicar. Had he not been protected by their outward angelic appearance, his dwindling supply of grey hair would have stood on end! From personal knowledge all the boys in the choir were very involved in a nocturnal activity known as 'mischief nights', November 4th being the highlight. Black cotton thread would be tied to a door knocker as the perpetrators, protected by the 'black-out', hid across the street. Two tugs on the thread manifested some 'mysterious person' who knocked on the door which, when opened, revealed only the cold November night air. These activities, plus other tales of 'daring-do' would, I am sure, have caused the Vicar to pray for the souls of his wayward flock of (apparently) 'angelic' choir-boys!

Following a long sermon it made me realise that the pews were not built for comfort. It was a relief when we had to stand for two more hymns followed by a psalm. I had to admit that I always felt a sense of relief when the Vicar gave his final blessing and we could vacate our rock-hard pews. As I had observed in the past, the choir formed up in pairs and being led by the same senior member of the choir and headed by the Vicar wearing the same solemn expression, the procession filed past us and entered into the vestry. The congregation now commenced to file down the aisle towards the exit, nodding and greeting friends as they did so. Near the doorway their short steps developed into a shuffle and finally halted as each member of the congregation waited to speak to, or to be spoken to by the Vicar who was standing just outside the church door. We joined the queue and slowly continued to shuffle until we emerged into the sunlight. Once outside I could easily overhear the Vicar greeting his parishioners, asking how family and sons were, and giving words of comfort to the bereaved. It was now our turn. In church I had noticed that the Vicar was wearing very thick spectacles and now that we were standing before him they looked more like the ends of jam jars! He was a tall, thin man with thin greying hair. He had a kindly face and, as Nellie introduced me, he gently shook my hand and smiled down at me from (to my eyes) his great height.

Nellie wasted no time about informing the Vicar of 'our' intentions.

"So, Alastair, you want to join the choir? Do you have a good voice?"

Before I could reply Nellie, acting as 'my agent', stepped in.

"Vicar, he sings like an angel. He sang a song t'uther day and it was beautiful!"

She looked down at me.

"What was it called?"

"It was 'Red Sails in The Sunset'."

I had visions of having to give an impromptu audition there and then, not only to the Vicar, but the remainder of the congregation waiting to exit the church! The Vicar came to my rescue.

"Choir practice is held every Wednesday evening commencing at six o'clock. If Alastair comes along then, the Choir Master will assess his suitability."

Nellie beamed and squeezed my hand.

"Vicar, thank you very much, Alastair will be theer."

There was no escape: With Nellie as 'my agent' there was no question of "if" I would be accepted; it was "when."

On the way home Nellie conducted the conversation in the future tense.

"When yer in t'choir, think how smart yer'll look in yer surplice and cassock. I'll get our Jack ter take yer photograph ter send home to yer muther. And think, at Christmas time yer could be singing solo!"

The Wednesday duly arrived and having been inspected from 'head to toe' by Nellie, I set off for the church, meeting on route two of my newly won school friends who were in the choir.

"So thars joining t'choir then?"

I nodded.

"I hope so, I'm having a test to see if I am suitable."

The tallest of the pair who was walking with his hands in his pockets said,

"'Ave yer bin told about t'pay?"

"No, how much is it?"

"Six pence a munth but, when people git married, t'bridegroom 'as bin known ter give us as mucch as two shillings each! Theer's nowt extra for funerals an' we don't git asked ter sing at them."

I recalled the 'rock hard' pews.

"What do you do when the Vicar gives his sermon? Do you find it boring?"

"Nay, we read comics. We stick them upp t'sleeve of t'cassock, then during t'sermon we slide 'em out."

I had no intention of letting Nellie know the secret life of the village choirboys!

I arrived, was introduced to the adult members of the choir, and tried my best to sing scales. This was followed by attempting to hit the notes given off by a variety of tuning forks. The Choir Master would strike a tuning fork on a hard surface, and then place the stem onto it, when it would give off a clear, high-pitched note. I had to try and replicate this note. I must have succeeded because – I was in!

Following choir practice, and before returning home to give Nellie her 'expected' good news, I was fitted with a cassock and a white surplice and requested to take the surplice home to be washed and ironed.

If my reluctant fight had given me ten plus points with Jack and Harold, then being selected to join the choir gave me twenty points from Nellie! As soon as Jack and Harold arrived home, they were given the good news.

"Our Alastair's int'Church choir!"

Thankfully Nellie did not mention my (expected) forthcoming Christmas solo performance. From his reaction to the news I had the feeling that my fight had impressed Harold far more than being selected to be a choirboy.

And so the Wednesdays and Sundays came and went. We (hopefully) 'sang like angels' and during the long sermons we read our comics. With the arrival of summer we had another distraction. In the churchyard a weed grew in abundance. It had long hollow stems that supported bunches of very delicate white flowers. Elderberries fitted perfectly inside the hollow stalk, thus providing us with 'home-made' 'blow-pipes. Armed with a stalk and some semi-ripe berries, during the long sermons it was possible to just poke the stalk through the hollows in the carvings on the choir stalls and 'fire' at your opponents in the choir stalls directly opposite. The ultimate 'accolade' was to be able to hit your opponent through one of the opposite apertures. As you will have realised, there were many misses. The end result was, upon completion of the service, elderberries that had fallen onto the aisle were being squashed underfoot as the Vicar and the choir filed out. It all came to a very rapid end! The adult members of the choir were not amused by our antics and informed the Vicar. This complaint, together with those of the cleaning ladies, resulted in the Vicar reminding us that we were in the 'House of God' who would not be amused by our behaviour! As a result we had to revert to comics.

With the end of summer it was time for the 'Harvest Festival'. As a choir we started rehearsing the traditional hymns and psalms. A few days before the 'Harvest Festival' there was a hive of activity within the church. Flowers and foodstuffs were constantly arriving at the church and being delivered into the arms of the numerous enthusiastic volunteers. The altar and the steps leading up to it, were bedecked with mounds of washed and carefully placed potatoes; greens and root vegetables; sheaves of corn; bread baked to a golden-brown and in the shape of a sheaf of corn; apples; pears; jars of jam and pickles and, even trays of eggs. On the altar itself, in front of the pulpit, the font, and in every conceivable place, there were 'mountains' of flowers. Within two days the interior of the church had been transformed.

On the afternoon of the Festival, as I walked down the hill with Nellie dressed in my 'Sunday best' dark navy-blue suit, the day felt very special. It wasn't only that it was a beautiful morning, or the choir's build-up and the activity within the church, but in less than an hour we would start singing the opening hymn – 'We plough the fields and scatter the good seed on the land......' During practice we had sung this hymn with gusto, but according to the Choir-Master, as this was a well known hymn the most 'gusto' would be provided by the congregation, therefore it was important that we, the choir, should be heard above the congregation and lead the singing. As I walked down the hill with Nellie, in my mind's eye together with the choir, as the organ played the first few opening notes I would stand and sing like I had never done before: "We plough the fields and scatter the good seed on the land......!

The church was packed. There were even more displays of flowers than when I had last visited the church the day before to attend our final dress rehearsal. There were flickering candles positioned on each side of the altar. Other large candles supported on tall ornate holders were on each side of the steps leading up to the altar, created an almost magical scene. At that moment in time I did not wish to be anywhere else. As I donned my black cassock and my pristine white surplice I felt very proud that I was a member of this village choir.

Headed by the same senior member of the choir holding aloft the large brass cross and followed by the Vicar, we filed out from the vestry with slow measured steps and into the choir-stalls. The Vicar knelt briefly in prayer, the organist sounded the first few notes, the choir and the congregation rose to their feet – and we all sang with gusto! "We plough the fields and scatter the good seed on the land......" The sheer volume of sound made my scalp tingle! As the service progressed and the light outside began to fade, the light from the flickering candles became more intense, adding another dimension to the occasion. Even being a temporary member of this Yorkshire village, and seeing all the good things that the many surrounding farms in the area had produced, as a child the words of that very special hymn meant a great deal to me. One has to have lived within a village surrounded by good farming folk to really appreciate what the aftermath of harvest time really means to farming people.

Following the service every item on display was made into parcels and we were given the names and addresses of the local poor people. Most of them were old and frail, some lived alone. It never failed to give me pleasure to knock on a door and hand over 'the goodness of the land' to very grateful – and sometimes tearful – recipients.

The next major event was Christmas. The build-up began weeks before as we sang the descants to the many Christmas favourite carols, such as: 'The Holly and the Ivy'; 'We Three Kings of Orient Are' and 'Oh Come All Ye Faithful'. The highlight was, just prior to Christmas Eve, going out in the snow to sing carols. Despite the 'black-out', to illuminate our path, we had one oil lantern (carried by the Vicar) and candles in disused jam-jars (carried by us). Our initial trek would take us to the big houses on the outskirts of the village, where we would sing two (shortened) carols. The snow would reflect the yellow and orange light given off by our lantern and candles, casting deep shadows all around us, and where the snow had gathered on bushes it caused it to sparkle. Our cold faces and rosy cheeks would be bathed in this same soft light. Christmas and all that it stood for felt so close you felt as if you could touch it!

The doors of the houses would be opened (normally by a maid), and we would be invited to step into the cosy warm hall to sing yet another carol. The owners and their wives would appear and make a generous donation. Sometimes we were invited into the kitchen where the cook would provide hot drinks and mince pies, or home made biscuits. Then it was out into the cold night air. As the snow crunched beneath our feet, we would place our gloved hands around the jam-jars for a modicum of warmth, as, led by the Vicar, we made our way to the next big house.

Following this initial excursion we would then tour the village, pausing from time to time to ensure that our carols reached as many ears as possible. People in the nearby houses would venture outside into the cold to add their donations to the Vicar's collecting tin. The climax of all this activity was Midnight Mass. Not only could we stay up late – way beyond our normal bed-time – but to experience the atmosphere within the ('blacked -out') church was very, very special. The flickering candles, the church bedecked in holly; the excitement as all our practice of the carols with their descants came to fruition. We sang with confidence and gusto, our shrill boys' voices singing in descant, rising and falling above the voices of the congregation. Mid-night Mass was always a wonderful start to Christmas.

At 'home' breakfast on Christmas morning was also special. The fire would be burning brightly as we all exchanged presents. I cannot recall what I gave or received, but from the expressions on our faces, everyone was delighted as the multi-coloured wrapping paper was removed. My very special presents and cards were from my mother and family. As I read each card and recalled their faces, I found it difficult to stem the tears. For Christmas dinner Nellie had excelled herself – despite rationing it was all there commencing with one of Harold's non-laying chickens in pride of place on the table! There was an addition that I almost forgot to mention. As he carved the chicken, Harold was resplendent in a collar and tie!

Throughout the year there were weddings; Easter to May being highly favoured months. As I had already been informed, bridegrooms were not averse to 'opening their wallets' – the norm being two shillings per choir-boy. 'Stingy' ones gave a shilling, and the very generous, two shillings and six pence. To put these sums into perspective, you may recall that we were only paid six pence a month. Therefore, the chance to earn at least double – if not more – for just half-an-hours singing, meant that there was never a shortage of volunteers!

During early autumn there was the choir-boys day out. The Vicar would take us by bus to the nearby town of Keighley for 'high-tea'. Remembering that rationing was in force, the fare was fairly basic. For example 'dried' egg on toast, (egg powder mixed with milk to make scrambled egg). As fresh eggs were rationed, dried egg powder from America was a very good substitute to make 'scrambled egg'. There were the inevitable potted meat sandwiches and 'tea-cakes', washed down with cups of hot, sweet tea. Despite the paucity of variety, we enjoyed every minute and every mouthful of the Vicar's 'high-tea'. The highlight was a visit to the pictures, (today we use the word 'cinema'). All the films were black- and- white. The film was normally a comedy with film stars such as Will Hay, who normally played a schoolmaster with an over-weight boy pupil who stumbled upon some German spy ring, or George Formby who always found some reason to play his ukulele and sing such songs as: "Mr. Wu Was a Laundry Man." The words included such phrases as: "he had a naughty eye that flickers; you ought to see it wobble when he's ironing ladies blouses, etc." Being young, the play on words didn't register and the Vicar must have been very embarrassed as, on the bus during the return journey, twelve choir-boys sang the song with all the words, which no doubt accounted for his shy smile to the conductress as he paid for our fares, and the grins of the older male passengers.

Within the choir strong bonds were formed. We sang together and played together within the village and its surrounding countryside. Later, upon my return to Brighton, I would miss the choir and my involvement in the various Festivals, but most of all, the sense of 'belonging' to a small Yorkshire village.

8. "I reckon them's cows."

With our teachers long departed, and our original class having been integrated into the village school – our 'ranks' started to thin. Despite the bombing and the overhead aerial battles, some parents travelled to Yorkshire to retrieve their children and take them back to Brighton. This was not a mass exodus. Over a period they left in ones and twos. We who remained had to rely more and more heavily on mixing with, and being accepted by the local children. Due to my unjustified reputation as a fighter, I had already been accepted into their midst, even the two 'toughs' who were in our class, were on friendly terms. It was about this time that, due to our ages, we were moved into a different class and came face to face with the lady English teacher who had the reputation of enjoying cracking pupils on the knuckles with a stick, if, in her opinion, their hand-writing was not up to her expected standard. I can remember her appearance. She was short in stature and over-weight; had dark short crimped hair and wore circular, black- rimmed glasses. Her chin had a hint of blue about it as if she shaved. Her eyes were dark brown and set in a fat, mean-looking face. I cannot recall her ever smiling. Hand-writing was her apparent raison d'être.

Commencing with our first lesson, sitting behind her raised desk, she spelt out her 'rules' for the class. Her dark beady eyes scanned every child. It was obvious that there was to be no jollity of any description. In her class we were there to perfect our hand-writing and learn the construction of English, which consisted of reading out aloud from various stories and poems.

Using the black-board and chalk, she started to write each letter of the alphabet in what we called 'joined-up' writing'. We were issued with ruled foolscap paper and pencils and told to copy her writing. There was utter silence – you could have heard a pin drop. With heads down, and with one arm crooked across the paper, we tried to copy the letters on the black-board. As we did so, she slowly walked up and down between the desks observing our tentative initial efforts. Having observed for a few minutes, she stood in front of the class and we were told to stop writing. There was not a trace of kindness in her face. Facing the black-board she pointed to each letter, stressing how the letters were formed and finished. She was not satisfied. We had to concentrate more and to start writing on a new line. Recalling her reputation I had a feeling of unease. Until now I had always enjoyed my lessons. The atmosphere in this English class was not conducive to learning. Before I started writing again, I quickly looked at the faces to my left and right. Their expressions matched mine – there was an element of fear.

As we again tried to copy the way she had formed the letters, again she walked up and down between the desks, this time holding a short stick and pausing from time to time to observe our progress. She stopped by one of the village boys.

"You are not looking at the board."

Each word was stressed with a light tap on his head with the stick. This did not augur well for the rest of the lesson. The pacing and pausing continued. Suddenly she stopped by one of the class 'toughs', looked at his work and cracked him on the knuckles with her stick.

"Hold your pencil properly!"

He made a sharp intake of breath and rubbed the knuckle of his right hand as she continued to stalk around the classroom.

She now stopped by a boy with fair hair that always looked as if it had never seen a comb. She looked down at his work and I had that horrible feeling in the pit of my stomach. Down came the stick onto his knuckles.

"You are not trying to write properly!"

"Please Miss, I am trying."

"Nonsense!"

And again she struck him across the knuckles of his right hand and he yelled with pain! He rubbed his knuckle and stood up.

"Miss, please don't 'it me agin, because if yer do I'll punch thee!"

All work stopped! This was unreal! What would happen? She lashed out at him with the stick and he punched her on the shoulder! Now, very red in the face, she again lashed out with the stick. As he backed away she pursued him round the classroom as he tried to avoid her growing level of fury. She cornered him near her desk and received another punch! The door burst open – it was the Headmaster! He grabbed the boy and took him outside. Minutes later we could hear the sound of the strap being used and the accompanying yells. I felt frightened and sick in my stomach. The door opened and the boy was led back into the classroom held by the 'scruff of his neck'. He was sobbing, the tears streaming down his cheeks. He was told to sit down. Everyone in the class, including me, had the strain of fear showing on their faces. The Headmaster faced us.

"If anyone hits this teacher again, they will receive a bigger thrashing than he has had."

He then strode out of the classroom. The lesson continued in utter silence. The teacher sat at her desk and it was obvious that she was breathing heavily and her stick was not in sight. When the lesson finished we returned our pencils and paper to her. No words were exchanged and she stood up and made for the door.

The boy was still crying and we all crowded around him to ask what had happened?

The answer was obvious to all. He looked down and shook his head.

"'E 'it me with t'strap and it wern't my fault."

One of the girls asked,

"Will yer tell yer Mum an' Dad?"

He looked at her with his tear streaked face and shrugged. At that very point in time there was only one place where I wanted to be – home with my mother and grandmother.

The instigator of this incident did not return to her class that day. We had been stunned and horrified by the whole affair. As children we would not have dared to report this sadistic woman. To us, teachers were all powerful and they controlled our lives from the moment we entered the school gates in the morning, until we departed again each afternoon.

To the members of our original group from Brighton, such sadistic behaviour was totally unknown. Our teachers were kind and considerate and we respected them. Corporal punishment of any kind was unknown to us, yet here in this village school use of the strap was commonplace. Following this incident even more members of our original group returned to their families, as, no doubt, letters had been sent home and as a result horrified parents had reacted. For some reason that I cannot recall, my mother was not made aware of how I felt, or that I wanted to return home. For a reason I cannot recall, I never mentioned it to Nellie.

Some weeks later it was rumoured that the English teacher was leaving and from memory she was replaced by a younger, kinder woman who had a totally different approach. So life returned to normal. I still collected the eggs, helped Harold with his rabbits and chickens, and attended Sunday school, choir practice and the church services. Also, with the passage of time I had developed some strong bonds with boys of my own age.

Two of my village friends were very keen on collecting birds' eggs and had strict rules – you only removed one egg from each nest. I was shown how to remove the yolk without damaging the shell. Using a pin, a small hole was made in the top and the base of the egg, then placing the lips close to one end and blowing very hard was all that was required before the egg could be added to the collection. This was a whole new world to me and I soon knew the difference between a blackbird's nest and a thrush's nest and that robins eggs were small, white and covered in tiny red spots. Curlew's eggs were naturally well camouflaged being a brown-green colour with dark brown flecks. So when I was invited to join them to search the moors for these eggs, I gladly accepted.

The following Saturday we set off to the nearby moor to search not only for curlew's eggs but also for pheasants eggs. Our route took us into a farm-yard where a large Billy- goat was on guard. We ignored the goat and continued towards the far gate. For some unknown reason it decided to trot up to me. As I went to pat it on its head, it lightly butted me in the stomach. As I backed away it lowered its head and gave me an even harder butt! By this time I had my back to a stone wall and the only way that I could protect myself was to hold onto its horns. To my complete surprise the horns were warm! I was now being pulled forward as the goat backed away, then being 'bashed' up against the stone wall. My two companions must have run off to report my forthcoming demise to the farmer, as a red faced, well built lady suddenly appeared with a broom. She told me to let go of the horns. As I did so, she hit the goat on the head with the heavy end of the broom! The goat stopped advancing on me and shook its head several times as if dazed. I swear that the goat went cross-eyed! With the goat still looking dazed, she gave it a shove on one of its shoulders. The goat took two sideways paces and continued to shake its head. She bent down and touched my shoulder.

"Are yer all reet luv? It's not t' first time 'e's dun that."

She looked at the back of my jacket.

"It's not torn or marked, now you runn along with yer friends."

As I turned to go she shoved the goat in the ribs with the head of her broom.

"Git off with yer!"

The goat, who was no doubt still dazed, moved slightly. We did not wait to see the outcome and quickly made our way to the moor. I must admit I was quite shaken and was very thankful that my companions had called for help.

"Bye ek Alastair, that goat could 'ave killed thee."

With the passage of time, slowly but very surely, I had adopted the Yorkshire dialect.

"Aye John, thar cud be reet."

My next encounter was with a somewhat larger animal. With two of my local friends we had gone roaming around the area and had reached a wooden gate. In the field some fifty yards away and happily grazing were about twenty cows. For some minutes we stood observing the herd as it was our intention to cross the field. I studied each animal in turn. I turned to my two companions.

"I reckon thems cows." I said confidently and commenced to climb over the gate. My two companions hesitated.

"Are thee sure?"

"Aye, cum on, climb t'gate. Thars not scared are thee?"

This comment goaded my companions into action and we commenced to cross the field to another gate on the far side. Our route would take us very close to the herd. It was a beautiful day as the cows munched the grass and flicked their tails to keep the flies away. Carefully avoiding the numerous results from their previous grazing, and with confidence that only three young boys out on a jaunt can have, we were drawing very close to this band of milk producers. Some of the cows looked up as we approached. On the far side of the herd, a 'cow' with a wide forehead, large horns and very broad shoulders, continued to look in our direction as, without a care in the world we made for the other gate. Our attention was diverted from our objective by this 'cow'. With its head raised it started walking towards us. Although the distance separating us was at least forty yards, we stopped. The following three words pumped adrenaline into our veins.

"It's a bull!"

I was to quickly discover that the old saying "fear gives you wings" is perfectly true! Our nearest refuge was a nearby tree which no doubt was used by the herd during the summer to shelter from the hot sun. As the bull broke into a trot we 'ran like the wind' and scrambled into the lower branches of the tree as the bull arrived below us. I do not know about my two companions, but my heart was going 'sixty- four to the dozen'! The bull looked up and snorted making me grip onto the branches even harder! Fear can have the following effect. The smaller of my companions said,

"I want ter go ter't lavatory!"

And the bull was directly below our refuge!

"Yer can't, bull'll kill thee!" came the desperate response.

I recalled a not so dissimilar predicament when I was in Bradford with Harold.

"Do thee widdle from t'tree."

My suggestion was quickly followed by the sounds of branches being disturbed, causing us to make loud shushing' sounds which was greeted by the sound of fluid hitting the ground below.

By now the bull had moved away from the base of the tree and was grazing about fifteen yards away. What were we to do? Any movement caused the bull to raise its head. Each time it did so the main thing I noticed was the size of its horns! By this time we had been up the tree for about fifteen minutes. The 'widdler' made a very apt remark.

"Bugger's not gayin away."

We sat in the branches as our would-be annihilator, with a nonchalance that only a grazing herbivore can have, held us captive in the tree. An hour must have passed.

The bull had moved further away, but was still 'too close for comfort'.

Would we have to stay up here all night? The bull had found some lush grass and the distance had now increased to perhaps thirty-five yards. Words of bravery started to enter into our exchange of ideas.

"If we climb down t'tree on opposite side, t'bull won't see us – then we'll run like 'ell t'gate!"

On balance, although this idea was not without merit, it was agreed that one of us would have to sacrifice his life to save the other two. Not surprisingly there were no volunteers. The next idea was even bolder.

"I've seen t'farmer 'it bull with a stick an' it moved off."

"Don't be dafft, where's t'stick an' I can't see thee being first down t'tree."

We continued to wait. Slowly but surely the bull moved towards his lady friends and suggestion number one was voiced again. We eyed the nearest gate and calculated that it was a good forty yards away. The bull by now was also a good forty yards away. As there was no house within shouting distance, and we would eventually starve to death, plan number one was put into action. As quiet as mice we moved round to the far side of the tree, waited and listened. All was quiet. We held a whispered consultation.

"'As bull moved?"

"Nay, I don't think so."

" 'Ow far's t'gate?"

"If we runn like 'ell by t'time t'bull see's us we'll be over t'gate."

We'd risk it! Now boys shorts have several shortcomings as was aptly demonstrated when sliding down the tree, the end of a small broken branch disappeared up the leg of one of my companions shorts, bringing his escape to a rapid halt! By now we were at the base of the tree and heard his plaintive whisper.

"I'm stuckk!"

"What's upp with thee?"

"Branch 'as gone up me shorts!"

"Then tek it out."

"I can't, I'll fall down!"

I very cautiously peered around the trunk of the tree. The bull was still happily grazing and had hardly moved. I returned to my earthbound companion.

"T'bulls all reet"

There was some rustling in the branches overhead which made the two of us to utter several "shss's." At long last a pair of clogs appeared and with our hands supporting his bottom, he was helped onto the ground. Again I cautiously peeped around the tree. The bull was still grazing! There was a rapid whispered conversation which ended with the words,

"Run fur t'gate!"

Had we been entered for the National Junior one hundred yard dash we would have won! I have never ever before or since, run forty yards and climbed over a farm gate with such alacrity! We were safe!

And what about the bull? He was still grazing very contentedly with his lady friends.

9. Carrots!

The war still continued and from time to time I would hear Nellie telling Harold that another mother was grieving for a son killed in action. Within the school some children failed to attend and when they did appear the word quickly spread that their Dad had been killed. At church the Vicar would mention the name of the father or son during the service, and ask us to include the wife or mother in our prayers.

Together with Nellie I sometimes listened to the B.B.C. news broadcasts about ships being 'lost'; the numbers of German aircraft destroyed; our bombing raids into Europe and Germany. As children, safe and sound in Yorkshire, apart from the 'Home Guard' in their army uniforms, or seeing the uniforms of servicemen on leave, the war hardly intruded into our lives. There was one main thing which did touch us – food rationing. However, Nellie never failed to produce good wholesome hot food. As I sometimes accompanied Nellie to the local Co-op and the butcher, I knew that the meagre quantity of food placed into Nellie's basket would just about cover a dinner plate. This paucity of food was supplemented by our plentiful supply of eggs, vegetables from the small allotment and, as I was to discover, meat from a very local source, which did not include 'my' favourite or 'the champion'. Some Sundays when we sat down to a roast chicken dinner, I tried not to remember the inert feathered source hanging upside down on a hook in the garden shed.

At this time the papers and the B.B.C. news broadcast the exploits and successes of Britain's night-fighter ace, Group

Captain 'Cats Eyes' Cunningham. His score of shot-down German planes, which had intruded into our air-space, mounted weekly. What was the secret of his success? Carrots! As soon as this became known, every schoolboy that I knew, each morning, when on the way to school, purchased a ha'penny carrot. In my case it was from the local Co-op which was on route. Prior to this, as oranges were no longer available, the population as a whole had been encouraged to eat raw carrots. I had to admit that within our family of four we did eat carrots as part of our normal diet, but never raw and certainly not in abundance. However, within days of 'Cats-Eyes" Cunningham's 'secret' becoming known, the local Co-op and greengrocer's, carrot sales escalated and the ha'pennies helped to 'swell' their coffers. So I commenced to improve my night vision. From now on carrots took on a new meaning. No longer did I look at the box of Co-op carrots in my previous off-handed manner. I became highly selective. Within seconds of standing before the box, my eyes would rapidly scan every visible carrot. Then, I would rake down deeper into the box to ensure that the carrot had not escaped my attention. Finally, I would select just two, comparing both the length and girth – finally discarding the 'loser'. Then, and only then, would I approach the wooden counter and part with my ha'penny. The lady behind the counter was very tolerant, as I was not the only school-boy seeking that extra large carrot. Her initial comments had been,

"Don't forgit ter wash it."

This changed to, "Oh, it's you again fur yer daily carrot."

And finally, "Don't tek all day luv, they're only carrots."

The lady was always pleasant but she obviously did not understand two things. Value for money, and when arriving at school, possessing the biggest carrot that a ha'penny could buy.

Once into the school playground carrots would be compared in order to establish who had achieved the best buy. Carrots were compared as if they were taking part in a 'conker' championship. Boasts of how their night vision had improved was commonplace amongst the boys. I must admit that I had not noticed any change. Night after night, having said my prayers, I would switch off my bedroom light, push the 'black-out' curtain to one side and peer out into the night. I always waited at least a minute for my eyes to adjust from the brightness of the overhead light. Was my night vision better than the night before?

So the ha'penny carrot sales continued and for some, exceeded the norm of one raw carrot a day. In order to have super night vision, a small group of boys at our school over indulged in the consumption of carrots and developed a distinct yellow tinge to their skins! The story that carrots were now being consumed by every RAF pilot was issued to cover-up that Britain had invented RADAR, whereby German aircraft could be detected on route to bomb our towns and cities. Their presence, speed and direction could be seen on small, round, glass screens (similar to a smaller version of today's televisions) and our fighter aircraft were then directed onto their formations.

Apart from carrots there were other sources of non-rationed food. Being in a farming area had its advantages. One week-end Nellie suggested that Jack and his girlfriend should take me to a local farm for 'high-tea'. Recalling that in Brighton, 'high-tea' always included cream cakes, I was very keen to go! My gastric juices were also stirred with stories of home-made bread; home-made jam, plus, farm produced bacon and eggs. I could hardly wait! As you now know, most of the basic rations were very small. Butter, lard, cheese, sugar, meat, tea and bacon were restricted to two ounces per item. Eggs, to anyone without chickens, were a rationed luxury. Fish and potatoes were not rationed, but were not always freely available. As a result, fish and chip shops, stocks permitting, which included the fat to fry in, could only open on an ad-hoc basis. Against this background the thought of being seated in a warm, cosy, farmhouse kitchen, listening to and smelling 'high-tea' being prepared was a tantalising prospect !

Jack and his girlfriend were joined by another young couple, and the five of us set off on foot for the farm, which was about three miles away. It was the type of afternoon that somehow you wished would never end. Dressed in our 'Sunday best', the warm sunshine caressing our faces, we strolled through meadows packed with wild flowers; cows with constantly twitching tails; the sounds of insects and birds. The two couples walked hand in hand and I walked next to Jack, who from time to time would draw my attention to various items of interest and sometimes posed a question.

"Them cows under t'tree are Ayrshires."

Or "Them tall pink flowers, do yer 'ave them in t'South?"

Jack having told the other three friends that I came from Brighton, they commenced to ask lots of questions and expressed surprise when I told them that in the summer the policemen wore white helmets. When I mentioned the size of the two piers and how far they extended out to sea, this prompted many more questions.

"Are yer safe when it's ruff?" Or, "Can yer buy ice-creams ont' piers?" And having answered their many questions...

"Alastair, this Brighton of yours sounds a reet good place ter live."

And so we continued our stroll at a leisurely pace with Jack and his friend exchanging banter with the two girls. Soon we neared the farmhouse.

The farmhouse was painted partly in white-wash, leaving a large proportion in its original grey stone. It was two storied with a slate roof and I noted that from its single chimney grey smoke rose into the afternoon air, to be dissipated by the very gentle breeze. To one side were some inter-connected single storey stone buildings attached to the end wall of the farmhouse. The door and window frames were painted a mid-blue. Beside the doorway was a 'spindly' pink climbing rose. The whole was surrounded by a low stone wall that led into a stone flagged yard. My overall impression was that it housed good stolid farming folk who lived and toiled the land as their forefathers had done before them. We opened the old five-bar-gate and entered into the yard. The only garden was a narrow strip on each side of the front door containing a variety of flowers, and the spindly rose which was supported by rusty wires attached to the wall. Having knocked on the door, we were invited in. Just off a short stone flagged passage, we entered a large kitchen, the floors being covered in the same worn stone as the passage. Against the far wall was a large black oven come hob on which stood a large blackened kettle. Outside it was still a warm day- in this airy kitchen with its wood-burning oven and despite the open window, it was 'roasting'!

The farmer's wife was, to my eyes, as old as Nellie. She was much shorter than Jack, had a ruddy complexion and unlike the two girls had a large waist. Her hair was tied into a bun and beneath her flowered apron she wore a black skirt. With her ruddy complexion and welcoming smile, had I been asked to draw a typical Yorkshire farmer's wife, here I had the perfect example. We were invited to sit at the large, well scrubbed kitchen table. The wooden chairs had high curved backs. Due to my size I could not rest up against the back support and I had to sit on the edge of my seat and rest my arms on the table. The walk had made me realise that I was hungry. The farmer's wife busied herself at the hob and then came over.

"I takk it yer want t'normal 'igh tea?"

We all nodded.

"Yes please."

"It's two fried eggs, with a slice of bacon, 'ome baked bread, jam an' tea."

She smiled and looked around the table.

"Yer realise t'bread 'as no butttter, an' theer's no sugar with t'tea, theer's a war on."

Leaving us she walked over to a rough wooden door and opened it. It was a very large pantry with stone shelves containing numerous jars of pickles and jams. Hanging from hooks in the ceiling, were two enormous sides of bacon. The lady returned to the hob carrying a plate containing eggs and several rashers of pre-cut bacon. I knew from conversations that Nellie had with Harold that farmers were also subject to rationing and any pig that was killed had to be authorised by the Government. A major portion of the pig, be it meat, bacon or ham, that was in excess of the family's requirements had to be handed over for public consumption. So how this farm was able to offer 'high-teas' was unusual to say the least! To a young boy with a generous appetite such thoughts never entered my head – we were about to have fried eggs and bacon!

The top of the hob was opened and a large blackened frying pan placed over the hole – food was on its way! I noted the cutlery set out on the table. Very few of the knives and forks matched. To the left of each fork was a mixture of side-plates. Somehow these odd items fitted perfectly in the warm, friendly farmhouse kitchen.

As we sat around the well-scrubbed table the farmer's wife continued to busy herself at the hob. Soon the kettle began to boil and within minutes a large brown earthenware teapot was placed onto the table, quickly followed by five large mugs and a jug of milk.. Having wiped her hands on a cloth, she said,

"Frying pan's nice an' 'ot, so bacon an' eggs wont be long."

We sipped our tea and waited. The farmer's wife returned and placed in the centre of the table several thick slices of bread and returned once again to the hob. One of the girls held out the plate to me and I took a slice. The bread was fresh and home-baked. Even without butter it tasted delicious! Suddenly from the hob came the sounds and the aroma of frying bacon, followed within minutes by the spluttering sounds as the eggs were dropped into the hot fat. There is something very special about the aroma of frying bacon and spluttering eggs! Soon five large white plates arrived, each plate with one thick slice of bacon and two eggs. I cannot remember which I tried first, but I do recall the bacon tasted very salty. No doubt due to the fat cooling down, the mouth watering aroma of frying bacon pervaded the whole kitchen. Perhaps it was because of our walk to the farmhouse, or that it was an idyllic day, the taste of that (illegal) salty bacon, remains with me to this day. Nothing was wasted. We wiped our plates clean with the bread. In this day and age of plenty such actions may appear to some readers to be uncouth, but unless you have known food restrictions, do not be too hasty to judge.

Our repast was now complimented with more fresh home-baked (unbuttered) crusty bread and a jar of home-made blackberry jam. As sugar was also rationed it never occurred to me to think where the sugar had come from. As a small boy with a large appetite, all I knew was that I would be leaving the farmhouse with a very full tummy. We drank our final mouthfuls of tea leaving the table bare, apart from a nearly empty teapot and an almost empty milk-jug. Jack and his friend settled the bill, we thanked the farmer's wife and set off to walk back to the village, feeling that the walk had been more than justified. Jack looked down at me.

"I bet yer don't git eggs an' bacon like that in Brighton."

I was feeling replete

"Aye Jack, thar could be reet!"

❖ ❖ ❖

You will recall that it was summer and by the time we left the farmhouse it was late afternoon. As we walked back towards the village the air was still warm and no doubt due to our full bellies our progress was somewhat slower. On route we passed through gates following the footpath across the fields. The two men and the girls walked hand in hand, stopping from time to time for a brief cuddle. After about a mile or so, Jack and his friends stopped and stretched out on the grass, the two girls joining them to enjoy the late afternoon sunshine. Jack and I had a wrestle, with Jack's friend shouting advice.

"Sit on 'im Alastair an' 'old 'im down!"

This was followed by many more tips on how to win. Finally I was declared the winner! As Jack and I lay back on the grass panting from our efforts, Jack remarked to his friend that I was a bit of a boxer.

"Is that reet Alastair? 'Ow about thee an' me 'aving a fight?"

Jack now added words of encouragement.

"Gay on Alastair, give 'im a thummp!"

In order to make sure that we were both about the same height, my 'opponent' knelt on the grass and put up his fists in a boxing pose.

"Cum on then Alastair, git the fists upp like this."

The girls were laughing and joined in.

"Thummp 'im Alastair!"

We sparred and he gave me a soft punch in the ribs.

"Cum on, show us what yer can do!"

He dropped his guard and I hit him Full Square on the nose! His head went back as the blood poured down onto his 'Sunday best' shirt, jacket and tie. He reached up and held a handkerchief to his nose.

"Bluddy 'ell, little buggers thumped me!"

His girlfriend was dabbing his nose with the bloodstained handkerchief and making sympathetic comments, adding,

"Jack did say 'e was a bit of a boxer."

I was mortified, not only had I hit him on the nose, I had ruined his clothes – and clothes were rationed!

I went over to my 'opponent'.

"I'm reet sorry, I didn't mean ter thump thee so hard."

Still clutching his nose and being tended by his girlfriend, he turned to Jack.

"This little bugger should be fighting t'Germans!"

He ruffled my hair.

"No 'ard feelings eh. We're still reet good friends."

With the bleeding under control a more subdued group set off once more for home.

Jack must have told Harold of my latest exploit, as he hugged me to him.

"Bye ek Alastair, I knew that thars a good un ter guard t'rabbits."

I felt very sorry for what I had done.

"Harold it was only in fun."

"Don't yer wurry lad, 'e'll git over it."

It was about this time that I witnessed the demise of one of Harold's chickens. Nellie had sent me over to the allotment to tell Harold that his dinner would be on the table in five minutes. I pushed open the shed door to see Harold holding a chicken by the neck which he then twisted and pulled. The chicken flapped its wings violently as Harold felt into his waistcoat pocket, produced a small curved-blade penknife and slit the chicken's throat. There was a gasp of air and its wings ceased flapping. Harold held it upside down by its legs, and then turned to me.

"'Ave yer not seen a chicken killed before?"

I shook my head.

"No Harold."

"Well Alastair she 'ad ter go as she 'asn't laid an egg fur ages. Now cum Sunnday when we all sit down ter a good chicken dinner, you eat upp. Just you feel t'weight."

Harold handed the dead chicken to me. Its legs felt warm!

"That's reet, hold on ter t'legs. Now theer's plenty of meat on 'er. Then cum Munday, wife'll make chicken stew, and if owt's left, we could be in fur sum chicken soup! Now I'll bet thar never 'ad that in Brighton."

I handed the dead chicken back to Harold noting the blood dripping onto the floor of the shed, its wings outstretched and lifeless. Harold took a piece of string from his pocket, tied the chicken's legs together, and then hung it on a nearby hook.

"Now, Alastair, if yer ever 'ave to kill a chicken, never chop its 'ead off. Do yer know why?"

I shook my head as in my mind's eye I saw the headless chicken and its flapping wings.

"Although it's dead, it'll runn around fur a few seconds."

That night having said my prayers, I climbed into bed and closed my eyes. Sleep was impossible – all I could think of was Harold's description of this headless chicken still being able to run around. All children have vivid imaginations, and the more I thought about the scene of the blood and this headless chicken, the more horrific and bizarre the scene became. Each night I always made sure my bedroom door was open. It took about a week before other things pushed this bloody vision into the back of my mind.

The following Sunday as Harold had predicted, following morning service at the local church, the four of us sat down to a very tasty roast chicken dinner.

I never did witness the demise of a rabbit, but when rabbit stew appeared on the table, there was no doubt in my mind that Harold's stock of rabbits was now minus one. In these days of plenty such acts of slaughter may seem barbaric. The sight of an animal being killed to satisfy human hunger is far removed from the minds of the people shopping at the butchers or the supermarket. They pick and choose from the plethora of meats, chickens, ducks and turkeys, now reduced to inert shrink-wrapped lumps of flesh. The choice is made and placed into the basket. 'What the eye doesn't see...'

10. Clogs!

Now you will recall that en route to my first day at the village school, Nellie had drawn my attention to the Clog Shop and had remarked, "That's where our Jack gets his clogs."

This had not really registered as I, like all the other evacuee children, wore shoes and it was not until we mixed in with the village children, who were also on their way to school, that I noticed everyone, without exception, wore this strange wooden-soled footwear. The boys' clogs were in the form of boots; the girls were more like shoes, some with small metal clasps to retain the instep firmly within the clog. Every clog was semi-pointed and had a small brass toe-cap.

I have failed to mention the noise that was made by this type of footwear. I was to discover that the soles of these wooden clogs were protected from wear by 'clog irons'. These irons were thin strips of metal attached to the outer edge of the sole and heel, then nailed into place with small nails. With scores of metal shod clogs coming into continuous contact with the pavements and tarmacadam roads, this very noisy clatter sounded very strange to our 'southern' ears! Now add to this level of noise the shouting of children running around the playground, or performing the girls' favourite pastime, skipping, and you will perhaps understand the auditory shock!

With the passage of time, and no doubt the increase in my shoe size – plus living within this small Yorkshire village, it will not surprise you that one day I would be persuaded to accompany Nellie to the Clog Shop. I recall asking Nellie if clogs were difficult to walk in as, unlike shoes, clog soles do not bend. Nellie's response had been, "Nay, not at all."

The Clog Shop was situated next door to the Co-op. The solid door was painted grey and it had a small dusty window in the centre of which was displayed a tiny pair of red leather clogs that must have been made for a two year old. To the left of these was a pair of black leather girl's clogs with the now familiar brass clasp. To the right was an enormous pair of black leather men's clogs. It occurred to me that it would not be overly difficult to convert them into a pair of toy sailing boats!

During the war all clothing and footwear was subject to 'rationing' which was achieved by a 'couponing' system. Everyone received the same number of coupons which were strictly controlled. For example, two shirts plus a set of underwear could absorb an entire annual allocation. Therefore, Nellie must have calculated that a pair of clogs would still leave sufficient coupons to purchase other essential items. I must admit I was not looking forward to having my feet thrust into a pair of clogs, despite Nellie's assurance that they would be warmer in the winter. So here we were outside this small shop with a reluctant 'shopper' and an expectant purchaser. Nellie opened the door and ushered me into the shop. My nostrils were immediately assailed by the smell of leather and wood. The shop had a wooden counter, part of which could be lifted to gain access to the workshop that was on view to its rear. The shop was deeper than its small exterior would suggest. Around the walls, hanging on a series of nails, were a whole range of clog and heel irons. Below these were racks of wooden clog soles. On the opposite wall hanging on long nails were pieces of black leather in various stages of construction. To the rear of the workshop was an 'over-sized' sewing machine and on another bench various sizes of metal clogs soles upper-most, with their hafts affixed into large wooden blocks. As we entered the shop the clog maker looked up, put down a small hammer and came over to the counter. He was of medium height, grey- haired and he wore round, steel-rimmed spectacles. He had on a dusty navy-blue apron with a long pocket at waist height. His kindly face reminded me of a thinner version of the toy-maker in Pinocchio! Having exchanged the usual greetings, Nellie wasted no time in explaining our presence.

"Our Alastair would like a pair of clogs."

The clog maker looked down at me.

"What size dus thar take?"

I shrugged my shoulders. Nellie 'stepped in'.

"Give t'gen'lman a shoe."

I bent down, quickly untied the lace and handed over my shoe. Not wishing to put my stocking foot on the floor, I was now standing on one leg and holding onto the counter for support. The clog maker studied the shoe very briefly, then returned it to me and indicated the solitary chair to the right of the counter.

"Sit down theer."

I was now faced with a decision – should I hop to the chair or, against my better judgement, walk 'peg-leg' fashion? I chose the former method and thankfully sat on the chair. The clog maker lifted the counter flap and placed on the floor three blank wooden soles. He lifted my stocking foot, examined it briefly and selected one of the wooden soles.

"Stand upp an' put yer foot on this."

Now clog soles are at least an inch or more thick. As a result I was now standing on one leg with my shoed foot off the ground. He looked up at me.

"How duss that feel?"

I was not overly keen to have a pair of clogs and standing on one leg did nothing to overcome my reluctance. I shrugged my shoulders.

Nellie posed the same question.

"How duss it feel? T'size looks just reet."

I shrugged my shoulders again. The clog maker noted my reluctance.

"You wait, int' Winter yer won't 'ave frozen toes with a pair of clogs on yer feet."

Nellie's words 'clinched the deal'.

"When will they be ready?"

From memory it was about a week, and I have no idea what the price of a pair of clogs was or the number of clothing coupons involved.

We left the shop. Nellie reached down and gently squeezed my hand.

"Yer first pair of clogs! Yer a real Yokshireman now!"

I was very glad that this would not include the almost obligatory flat cloth cap!

It was about a week later when, just as I was about to return to school for my afternoon lessons, Nellie called from the kitchen.

"I'll meet yer after school and we'll go and pick upp them clogs. I'll be waiting at t'gate."

My 'heart sank'. Clogs! All I could do was to make my usual reply,

"Aye, Nellie."

I walked down the hill with my mind 'full of clogs'. I had never ever worn boots and boys and men's clogs were always in the form of boots! The girls' clogs were more like shoes, but if I had insisted on a pair of those I would be looked upon as a real sissy. Another thought crossed my mind. As the winter was months away I could wear my shoes until it was really cold! Soon I joined the other children on their way to school and noted yet again the clatter of their clogs as the metal strips came into contact with the hard surface of the road and pavement. Before, I had only given a cursory glance at how the clog wearers walked – now I gave this my full attention. Unlike shoes, the solid wooden soles of the clogs didn't bend, so surely the only possible method was to walk 'flat-footed'? However, I was wrong. Everyone was walking 'normally'. I also realised that clogs added at least an inch to everyone's height. Despite this 'bonus' I was still very reluctant to have my feet shod in a pair of clogs made in unyielding black leather and shaped like a semi-pointed boot.

As promised, Nellie met me at the school gate. She gave me a beaming smile.

"Did yer enjoy school ter day?"

I responded with a simple "Aye".

Nellie reached down and squeezed my hand.

"Wait until Harold and our Jack see yer in yer first pair of clogs!"

We walked past the pie shop, turned right and walked towards the Co-op and the clog shop, where we turned left. Nellie led the way and opened the grey-painted door. As before, the clog maker was busy at the rear of the shop. He was holding a pair of pincers and removing the metal strips off the wooden soles of a pair of clogs and discarding them into a metal bin. He looked up and wiped his hands on the front of his apron.

"So yer've cum for t'clogs?"

He came forward and reached underneath the counter and placed a pair of brand new clogs on top. They were black with the usual brass metal toe cap. He gestured at the solitary chair.

"Tak a seat an' yer can try them on."

I picked up the clogs, they felt very heavy and I noted that the 'clog irons' attached to the wooden soles were shaped like a very shallow 'u', the prominent metal edges thus protecting the holding nails driven into the bottom of the 'u'. The heel irons were of the same construction. Removing my shoes I slipped my feet into the clogs and tied the leather laces. My feet were now encased in a pair of stiff black leather uppers and a pair of solid unyielding soles! I looked up at Nellie.

"They feel very stiff."

Nellie smiled.

"Bye yer look like a real Yorkshire man now! Stand upp and give 'em a try."

In standing the clogs felt and looked like deep-sea diver's boots! I made my first tentative steps. Walking as one would in shoes was impossible. Surely the only possible method was to walk 'flat-footed'? I looked at Nellie.

"How do I walk in these?"

Nellie 'tut-tutted'.

"Walk as you normally would."

I took another few steps. I turned to Nellie.

"They hurt around my ankles."

The clog maker had been watching my 'performance'.

"All yer need is sum dubbin. Let it soak in overneet an' they'll be nice an' soft."

Despite his assurance, they still felt like diver's boots!

Nellie added, "I'll get our Jack ter give 'em a good brushing with this 'dubbin' stuff."

With these words I realised my fate was sealed – 'like it or lump it' I now had a pair of clogs. Nellie parted with the money for the dual purchase and the clothing coupons. She looked down at me.

"Yer might just as well keep 'em on and I'll carry yer shoes!"

I 'clomped' my way to the door and we set off for home.

Unlike my shoes the clogs clattered with ever step. Had I been wearing my brown sheep-skin jacket I would have turned up the collar. If you have never worn unyielding, wooden-soled shoes or boots, then you have no idea how difficult it is to walk 'normally'. Place the edge of the heel onto the ground and take a 'normal' step. The solid wooden sole (obviously) doesn't 'give' and therefore one's foot is 'rolled' into the point of the clog. So this was why clogs had small brass toe-caps! I walked beside Nellie as I clattered on my way, semi-flat footed and feeling that all eyes were upon me. Nellie looked down at me

"So how's yer clogs?"

"They're very stiff and difficult to walk in."

Nellie smiled.

"When our Jack's finished with them, like the man said, they'll be nice and soft. You wait, in a few days yer'll wunder why yer ever wore shoes!"

Despite Nellie's predictions, plus several applications of dubbin, the upper – like the soles – remained unyielding.

Arriving home, and despite the fact that I was wearing grey woolen knee-length socks, the edges of the clogs had made red marks around my ankles. Removing the clogs I pointed these out to Nellie. She 'tut-tutted'.

"Don't forget yer haven't worn clogs before. I'll get our Jack ter give 'em an extra going over."

With Jack's arrival he was greeted with the words,

"Our Alastair's a real Yorkshire man now; he's got a pair of clogs just like yours!"

Jack grinned and gave me a wink.

"When yer go back ter Brighton, yer can tell 'em, these clogs came all the way from Yorkshire."

Upon my eventual return home I cannot recall what happened to my clogs. Perhaps they remained where they were made – in Yorkshire.

Later, Harold was also given the 'good news'. I seem to recall that his response was,

"Bye ek Alastair, now yer a real Yorkshire man!"

And so I became a 'clog wearer'. Jack did his best with the dubbin brush, with very marginal results. By trial and error I discovered that by not lacing the clog to the top of the last eyelet the rubbing around my ankles ceased. As clogs do not bend above the instep, the black leather could be brushed and polished to produce an amazing shine.

You will recall that when I had visited the clog shop, the man was removing the metal strips from the soles and heels with pincers. As a result, the wooden soles never wore out. Clog repairs were quick, easy, and completed in minutes. Off came the 'clog- irons', the previous nail holes were filled with discarded matches, the new 'irons' positioned and nailed into place – and that was it!

The first day that I wore my clogs to school, it was immediately noticed.

"I see thars got sum clogs then!"

With these words I realised that now I had really 'joined' the boys!

11.   Village activities

Although the church provided the main focus point for the village, there were other activities that provided both spectacle and enjoyment. With the snows of winter fast disappearing, spring was only weeks away. The first spectacle of interest was provided by the village Fire Brigade. Now, if the previous two words have conjured up images of a red fire engine, topped with a long ladder and announcing its presence with the ringing of a large brass bell – with blue uniformed figures resplendent in large brass helmets clinging to its sides – then you are about to be disappointed. The village 'Fire Engine' was manned by volunteers who wore army steel helmets painted white, and on the front of the helmet was displayed the letters 'A.F.S' which stood for 'Auxiliary Fire Service'. They wore dark navy-blue one-piece uniforms (rather like a 'boiler-suit') and around their 'middles' a wide black webbing belt from which hung an axe covered with a webbing sheath. It will come as no surprise when I tell you that every member was grey-haired!

I now come to the 'Fire Engine'. From memory it was very small, carried a short extendable ladder, and was painted a dull green. On its sides was the inscription 'Auxiliary Fire Service'. Attached to the rear was a two-wheeled trailer which housed a petrol engine that drove a pump. The pump could be connected by a hose to the nearest water source to suck up water. Under pressure the water to the actual hose could be directed at the fire. The fire hoses were carried in the rear of the 'Fire Engine', and, as you would expect, in rolls.

We now come to the first spectacle. With the advent of spring, birds of all shapes and sizes seek a mate, make a nest, and the female lays several eggs. Having sat on these for several weeks chicks appear. The Government decided that some birds had voracious appetites far in excess of their smaller cousins. Springtime was seed sowing time and seeds, particularly wheat, oats and barley, had not been sown to provide bird-feed. As we were at war, every scrap of land that could grow food was precious. However, this was not understood by the larger birds – namely rooks, crows and wood-pigeons. In order to protect grain crops from their voracious appetites, action was urgently needed and, who better to provide this than the grey-haired volunteers of the village 'Fire Brigade'.

It was a Saturday morning when I first heard the 'news'.

"Fire Brigade is squirtin' t'crows by t'church!"

Together with my two companions we hastened towards the church.

A small crowd had gathered, consisting mainly of young boys. The 'Fire Engine' was parked on the side of the road and the water pump with its trailer was going 'sixty- four to the dozen' and a long white hose was being held by two members of the A.F.S. who were directing a jet of water up into the air at the numerous crows nests. What goes up has to come down and, as a result, a torrent of water was falling from the trees, together with broken nests and scrawny, bald-headed chicks with large stunted beaks and bulging eyes. Circling above the trees the crows were 'voicing' their displeasure and below several boys were running through the continuous deluge and being soaked. Despite members of the A.F.S. shouting at them to stop, and despite the falling debris, their 'game' continued whenever an opportunity presented itself. No doubt their mothers would also shout when they arrived home soaking wet and filthy dirty!

With the water turned off, the next step was to ensure the demise of the numerous chicks. This was achieved by the four members of the A.F.S. 'donking' them on the head with sticks. Some of the boys joined in, and within minutes scores of corpses littered the wet, twig-strewn ground. Not surprisingly the crows 'cawing' increased in intensity! The 'show' was now over. The A.F.S. rolled up the lengths of hose, attached the trailer to their small fire engine and departed. I have no idea who cleared up the mess, but on my way to church the following day not a vestige remained.

The next major event was the 'Village Fête'. This was held in the grounds of the local Manor House which was within a 'stone's throw' of the church and housed one of my evacuee colleagues. No doubt due to its standing within the village, this was why it was our 'first port of call' when we set off on our rounds singing Christmas carols! The fête was held in the summer when the gardens were at their best. I had no involvement in the preparation of the fête, but I was conscious of the constant 'to-ing' and 'fro-ing' when attending choir practice. However, one member of the family was involved. Jack was to appear with several members of the 'Home Guard' to display an assortment of weaponry.

The day of the fête, a Saturday, duly arrived. Prior to our departure for the fête, Harold and I had been inspected from head to toe. Jack had not escaped. Despite stressing that he was in a hurry and had to join his colleagues, he was also inspected and given a 'flick' with the clothes-brush! Now it was our turn! Harold was told to adjust his tie and cardigan, and I was sent upstairs for my comb. Finally, we were both 'given a flick' with the clothes-brush. Nellie looked in the mirror above the fire-place and, having turned her head from side to side and adjusted her straw hat, patted her hair.

"Reet, we'll be off."

Once outside, Nellie locked the door and placed the key into her handbag. She turned and faced Harold.

"I don't want yer staying in the beer tent all afternoon."

Harold looked at me and raised his eyes skywards.

"If I do it'll be only fur a quick wun."

Nellie gave a little snort.

"Yer've said that before. Now let's be off."

We were all wearing our 'Sunday best'. Harold looked very smart in his collar and tie, plus a new flat cloth cap. Nellie was dressed in a smart navy-blue coat made from smooth material and, the most striking thing was her broad-brimmed straw hat that matched her coat. It suited her and I much preferred it to the narrow brimmed variety that she normally wore.

Arriving at the bottom of the hill, and before we turned left to make our way towards the church, the faint sounds of music could be heard. I looked up at Nellie.

"Will there be a brass band?"

The reason for my question was that I had heard brass bands on the wireless. A famous one was 'The Black Dyke Mills Band'. Nellie smiled and shook her head.

"Yer'd have ter go ter Keighley, they have a band theer."

As we drew closer I realised it wasn't a brass band, it had to be a gramophone, as I recognised the words of the song: "We'll meet again one sunny day...." This was a popular song that was often on the wireless. The song finished and an 'Announcer's' voice was heard inviting people to visit the various stalls.

By now we had arrived at the main road, and beyond the church I could see the flags and buntings. Rising above these was a large 'Union Jack' stirring in the breeze. Nellie turned to Harold.

"Don't forget what I said about the beer tent and don't forget our Jack is here."

Harold raised his eyes skywards.

"I've promised it will only be a quick wun."

Nellie gave another little snort.

"And don't forget it!"

It was obvious Harold was to be kept on 'a tight leash'!

We entered through the large gates and Harold paid our modest entrance fee. Ahead, spread across the lawn in front of the Manor House, were all sorts of stalls manned mainly by ladies all wearing large-brimmed hats of various colours and pretty patterned cotton dresses. Nellie looked down at me.

"Have yer got yer pocket muney?"

I nodded.

"Yes, Nellie."

Harold felt in his trouser pocket.

"'Ere lad, 'ave this."

He handed me a whole silver sixpence. As this represented one month's 'choir' money I was over-joyed!

"Thank you Harold!"

Nellie added,

"You gay off and find yer friends. I'll gay off with Harold to see our Jack."

I made to leave as Nellie added,

"Enjoy yerself, but don't waste yer muney!"

I wandered around the various stalls; the gramophone continued to play favourite songs; the flags and buntings stirred in the gentle breeze; everyone was in a happy mood. I 'spotted' the Vicar walking around stopping and talking to people. He wore a straw trilby hat; his usual 'dog collar; a black shirt without any buttons; a cream linen jacket; black shoes and black trousers. Being tall he was easily seen, being head and shoulders above the crowd. I met up with some of my friends.

"'Ave yer tried t'bran tubb?"

I shook my head.

"Is it good?"

My friend in the grey suit felt in the pocket of his jacket.

"It costs a penny a go an' look wot I've got!"

He produced a small cardboard packet containing ten wax crayons.

"Int' shops yer'd pay at least fourpence fur ten crayons. Go 'an 'ave a go!"

We walked over to the bran tub and I handed my penny to the lady in charge. She smiled.

"Yer can only 'ave wun go fur a penny. Put yer hand deep down in t'bran an' feel around. Everything is wrapped upp in newspaper ter hide the shape. Don't forget, once yer've pulled yer hand out yer can't put it back."

As directed I put my right hand deep into the tub. There were numerous wrapped parcels, some very small, others felt bulky. I moved my hand around and decided to go for one of the bulky items. My fingers made contact. I felt it all over. It had to be incredible value for a penny! I withdrew my hand clutching my prize! What could it be? I hurriedly tore off the newspaper.....It was a mug! The lady smiled.

"Yer've dun well for a penny."

It wasn't new but well worth a penny! I had to go and show Harold and Nellie!

After searching around I found Harold and Nellie near the tea tent.

"Look what I've got from the bran tub!"

Nellie gave it a cursory glance.

"At least it's not chipped."

I was still excited about my second-hand mug.

"It's well worth a penny!"

Nellie looked at my 'Sunday best' suit.

"Yer've got dusst all over that sleeve of yours, cum here and I'll brush it off."

With my suit restored to its original pristine condition, I left the mug with Nellie and ran off to find my friends.

Next to the tea tent was a marquee. To enter cost a penny – but what was inside? It was obviously very popular as it was full to overflowing with people. We parted with our money and entered. On each 'wall', and set at various levels, were pictures drawn in pastels and covering a whole range of subjects depicting the Manor House and its' grounds. A tall, elegant lady approached and spoke to us without a Yorkshire accent.

"So what types of pictures do you boys like?"

Noting my 'Southern' accent she said,

"We have one of your friend's staying here."

She pointed at some of the pictures.

"All these were drawn by the owner of the Manor. Let me show you one."

We stopped before a picture of a thrush's nest. Inside the nest were three pale blue speckled eggs. The nest was in a rhododendron bush. The lady looked down at us.

"Now do you think you could find this very bush?"

We shrugged our shoulders. The lady continued.

"If you can find it, tell me where it is and if you are correct everyone will receive a penny."

We could hardly wait! We scoured every rhododendron bush. Within fifteen minutes we found it. The nest was empty, but there was no mistaking it. It was just as it was depicted in the pastel drawing. It is something that has remained with me over the years. We ran back to the marquee and having been recognised by the old man on the entrance we were allowed to enter and found the lady. She smiled.

"Well?"

"We found it Miss!"

We described where we had seen the nest.

"It was just like the picture Miss!"

Having thanked the lady, we departed with our rewards.

Around the 'Home Guard' stand was quite a large crowd consisting mainly of boys, who were admiring a man in 'Home Guard' uniform who was sitting behind a machine-gun. Standing beside him was a grey-haired Officer who was stating its rate of fire, the distance it could fire, and finally that it was ideal for use against attacking infantry. He turned and pointed with his short, brown, leather-covered stick to a slim khaki coloured tin which was connected to the machine-gun by a slim hose.

"Due to its high rate of fire it becomes very hot; therefore it has to be cooled with water surrounding the barrel. Any questions?"

A boy, who was not in our class, put his hand up.

"Can it shoot down aeroplanes?"

The officer gave a perfunctory nod.

"It could, but as I've said its main use is against attacking infantry. Any more questions before we go on to demonstrate the rifle?"

Another boy raised his hand.

"What about tanks?"

The officer's voice changed.

"As I've already said, the machine-gun is designed for use against attacking infantry. The main infantry weapon is the .303 rifle…"

As Jack wasn't on the stand we left as the officer was extolling the virtues of the rifle to a large group consisting mainly of eager-faced young boys.

Having walked around the various stalls and attractions, and remembering the extra penny in our pockets, we were attracted to the 'White Elephant' stall. The table was laden with a whole host of items ranging from a brooch, pairs of cups and saucers; one or two well used toys, to half-a-dozen eggs. Every item had a numbered ticket. In the centre of the table was a large ceramic mixing bowl containing masses of screwed up tickets. The lady manning the stall told us it cost a penny to enter and every ticket won a prize! This was almost too good to be true! We each parted with a penny. I placed my hand into the mixing bowl, noting that it was impossible to see the numbers, so I chose mine from deep in the centre of the bowl and removed one ticket. The lady stepped forward.

"Open it to see what yer've wun."

I did so. I cannot recall the number of the ticket, but I had won a wooden pencil. My companions didn't fare much better. Their tickets won a comb and a small religious picture. We decided that the pencil and comb were good value for a penny, but the picture was a 'bit of a swiz'.

The flags and buntings continued to flutter in the gentle, warm breeze; the gramophone continued to play popular songs; people and children were going from stall to stall, some clutching various prizes, and the Vicar could be seen talking, smiling and nodding to his flock. We next tried 'hoop-la'. We didn't win a thing! As a result, not seeing anything that appealed, my friends decided to find their mothers and, in my case, Harold and Nellie. I found them coming out from the tea tent. They both waived and came over. Nellie asked,

"Well, did yer win ought else and did yer see our Jack on his stand?"

I produced my pencil and said although I had visited the 'Home Guard' stand Jack was not 'performing'.

With Nellie still clutching my mug we wandered around the various stalls and attractions. I pointed out the marquee that contained all the pictures, adding that I had, with my two friends, won a penny there and then the 'White Elephant' stall and the Bran Tub, saying how I had enjoyed myself. The day ended with everyone singing a very popular song. I can still remember the words:

"There'll always be an England and England will be free, if England means as much to you as England means to me. Red white and blue, what does it mean to you? Shout it aloud, stand up and be proud, England's awake! Etc.

This was followed by the National Anthem which was sung with gusto and fervour.

And so the day ended. The Vicar gave a brief speech, reminding us of those who were away fighting the enemy and also reminding us of those who would never return. I noticed some of the ladies were wiping their eyes. He concluded with a prayer. I cannot remember the words but, the combination of the prayer followed by everyone singing the 'National Anthem' made my scalp tingle! I felt very proud to be British! Nellie looked down at me and gently squeezed my hand. Looking up at her I noted that she too would need to wipe her eyes. I felt very proud of my Country. Yes, there would always be an England!

We left the fête in a sombre mood. Even Harold was not his usual buoyant self. Perhaps due to Nellie's 'tight leash', he hadn't visited the beer tent!

POLEGATE,
COUNCIL INFANTS SCHOOL,
EAST SUSSEX

Author 3 rd from right, front row.

The author, summer 1935.

The author at Polegate, Sussex 1937.

Brighton before the war. The author extreme right.
Centre is my cousin Bob with Aunt Ivy.

The author as a choir boy, 1941.

Nellie, her son Jack and the author.

Harold and Nellie, 1939.

Helping Nellie feed the chickens.

12.   There's nowt like a trout

You may recall that further up the hill from where I was living were a series of large reservoirs. According to my village companions, the first two contained enormous trout. To a group of young boys, tales of such magnitude demanded investigation.

It was a beautiful warm summer morning as the four of us set off, spurred on by 'our leader's' description of not only the number of trout, but their sheer size! After about a mile we turned off the road, climbed over a gate and there was the first reservoir. It was large and the water unruffled by any breeze was like a mill pond. Drifting on the surface were patches of pollen that must have come from the line of trees on the far bank. Our 'leader' had obviously been here before.

"See them trees over theer, down below is t'beck that runns down ter t'village. Theer's more trout in theer. They 'ide under t'rocks and yer 'ave ter tickle 'em."

We walked to the edge of the reservoir. There as far as the eye could see were enormous trout! The sight of these trout swimming lazily around and occasionally rising to the surface to swallow some insect, presented an irresistible challenge! I am not talking about the 'odd' trout; I am talking about dozens and dozens! It never occurred to me to enquire if we were on private land; the sight of so many trout blanketed any such thoughts. Now seeing all these trout was one thing, how could we catch them? We walked around the edge of the reservoir and again spurred on by 'our leader's' tales of more trout, we crossed several fields to the second cornucopia of trout. This reservoir was about the same size, almost devoid of trees and as we peered down into the water, not so many trout. We sat on the bank, throwing the 'odd' small stone at the fish and watching the ripples spreading across the surface. We discussed how we could catch one or two to take home. The only possible method was to use a fishing rod. We continued to explore the area until 'our leader' announced,

"We'd best be gayan 'ome fur us dinners."

On the way back down the hill the discussion continued. The consensus was, as no one had a proper fishing rod, we'd have to make them ourselves. We agreed to continue with our plans during school playtimes and, if it wasn't raining, to get together the following Saturday morning.

During the week our plans were finalised. Our 'fishing rods' could be fashioned from thin sticks. We could use bent pins for hooks, and black thread for the 'line. It never entered our heads that as it was war-time, black thread was not available for small boys to tie onto their 'fishing rods'.

The weather held and Saturday duly arrived. We had previously agreed that everyone would bring two pins to convert into hooks, the second pin being a spare. To avoid being pricked the pins were 'threaded' into the lapels of our jackets. At this stage we assumed that the Co-op was the obvious place to obtain a reel of black thread for the lines. After much discussion we decided that to fashion any type of fishing reel was beyond our abilities. As a result, we decided to tie a length of thread to the tops of our 'fishing rods'. The bait would be earth-worms that could be found under stones close to the reservoir. So, apart from the thread and the 'fishing rods', our equipment was almost complete. Arriving at the Co-op with our pooled resources we asked for a reel of black thread. The lady behind the counter looked at our eager faces.

"Is this fur thee muther?"

As 'our leader' was holding our pooled resources, we looked to him to respond. Obviously he did not wish to tell a lie.

"Nay Miss, it's fur fishing."

"Fishing! Black thread is like gold-dusst. We can't part with a whole reel of thread fur fishing. 'Ow muccd do yer need?"

Our 'leader' held his arms wide apart.

"About this mucch Miss."

She smiled.

"In that case yer best bet is ter ask yer muther."

We left the Co-op with our planned fishing trip in ruins. However, our 'leader' was not to be thwarted.

"I'll gay and ask me mum."

Within five minutes he was back with a whole reel of black cotton, saying that he had to promise to return the reel and to ensure that we could only use about five feet each. And so we set off for the reservoir.

The 'rods' were cut from carefully selected sycamore sticks about four feet long and the bark was then removed with a penknife. The 'fishing-lines' were restricted to roughly five foot lengths and tied to the tips of our 'rods'. The pins were bent into the shape of a hook. For floats, we cut three inch lengths from a thin sycamore stick and partly split each end. The 'floats' were set about eighteen inches from the 'hooks', the thread being inserted into a split, then wound around the 'float' a few times, then inserted into the other split. We were almost ready to fish. Now we needed bait. Lifting stones near the edge of the reservoir soon produced a number of wriggling earth-worms. These poor hapless creatures were then impaled onto our bent pins. We spread out along the bank, and then crouching low, we each made a cast. The worm and the hook sank below the surface.

Within seconds I could see several large trout approaching! Would they take the bait? Suddenly all four 'floats' disappeared under the surface and just as quickly reappeared. We pulled in our lines. The worms had gone! Once again we impaled four hapless creatures onto our bent pins and cast again. Within seconds the 'floats' vanished under the surface and again quickly reappeared. Once again we pulled in our lines. As before all four 'hooks' were bare. Looking down into the water the original number of trout had been joined by at least twelve others! I realised that as soon as the float dipped under the surface I should strike! With so many fish crowding around my 'hook' I couldn't fail to catch at least three or four big ones! Our exchanges conveyed our growing level of excitement!

"Bye ek, there's duzens of 'em 'ere!"

"Cor, look at the size of this wun!"

"Quick, let's find sum more worms!"

We all re-baited our 'hooks' and cast once again. I intended to watch my 'float' very carefully, but before I could do so the 'float' had disappeared and reappeared within seconds. I lifted the hook clear of the water – as before it was minus the worm. My three companions had also failed to hook a fish. My interest was kept at fever pitch when someone remarked,

"I could feel it wriggling an' it bent me rod!"

I lifted more stones and found more worms. I continued to cast, striking as soon as the float disappeared. By now there were dozens of large trout around the area where I was casting; some were even breaking the surface in expectation of more juicy earth-worms. Surely it was impossible not to catch one. By around mid-day we stopped 'feeding' the trout and tucked into the sandwiches provided by our respective households. During this time we discussed tactics.

"If we put t'float' closer ter t'hook, we'll see t'trout' swallow t'worm. A quick pull omt' line an' 'e'll be'ooked."

This seemed to be a very good idea.

"'Ow deep should we set t'hook?"

After much discussion we settled on twelve inches.

So, we found more worms, impaled them onto our bent pins and, having adjusted our 'floats' twelve inches from our bait, cast again. Within seconds of the 'hook' and 'float' landing on the water the trout reappeared, soon to be joined by many others. I could clearly see the worm wriggling on the hook. A large trout approached. I gripped the 'rod' ready to strike. In a flash the worm was gone! It was so fast that I had insufficient time to act! However, next time I would be ready!

By mid-afternoon all we had achieved was an assembly of at least fifty or more eager trout, who were now rising to the surface in anticipation of yet another four very tasty morsels. Our enthusiasm was beginning to wane. One of my companions voiced our thoughts.

"Them trout's reet greedy bugggers. Let's go 'ome."

We sat at the edge of the reservoir watching the circling and rising trout. To drown our sorrows we each took a 'swig' from the large bottle of 'Dandelion and Burdock'. All thoughts of taking home several big fat trout had, just like our live bait, vanished. We sat on the bank facing the prospect of a 'footloose' afternoon. One of my companions named Tom said that he had a good idea.

"Let's go down t'beck, I bet theer's sum big bugggers in theer."

The 'beck', which back in Brighton I would have referred to as a 'stream', was situated down the steeply wooded slope and just to the side of the reservoir. It meandered down to the village in a series of rock strewn runs and small pools. As it entered the village it was no more than six to seven feet wide and no more than thigh deep. As the water was 'crystal clear', checking it for trout was a good suggestion, so we abandoned our original 'expedition'. As we carefully made our way down the slope using bushes and low branches for support, below us I could both see and hear the rushing water, and where it plunged into the pools the water flashed as it 'caught' the afternoon sunlight.

Soon we all arrived at the beck. The noise of the running and cascading water was surprisingly loud. Our 'leader' had obviously done this type of fishing before. He bent down and studied the pool of flowing water. It was about fifteen feet long by about ten feet wide and no more than knee deep at its shallow end. The pool was being fed by fast flowing water cascading into its deep upper end. As I looked up and down the beck, what I was seeing was repeated in both directions. Our 'leader' stood up. He pointed.

"Trout git under t'stones."

He jerked his head at his nearest companion and then at us.

"We'll stay on this side an' you two go ont' tuther side."

Stepping carefully on the stones above the pool we crossed to the opposite side and commenced our search. All four of us bent down peering into the pool. At its lower end it was no more than twelve inches deep. From here it flowed in a series of shallow 'stony' runs into another pool. Some of the stones were more like boulders and impossible to even move. We had hardly gone more than ten yards when my companion knelt down and placed his hands under the edge of a large stone. As he did so, a large trout darted out from underneath and shot across to the other side disappearing from sight. We could not contain our excitement! We shouted.

"We've got wun an' he's shot over ter your side!"

Tom, who had suggested we try the beck, took charge of operations.

"Quick, git stones an' dam upp bottom end of t'pool!"

With feverish haste we complied with his orders as he and his companion did the same where the water was feeding out. Our feverish haste was accompanied by much splashing and thuds as stones were hurriedly removed from the beck and repositioned. The height of our 'dam' increased! There were more orders!

"Git sum sticks an' I'll keep me eye on t'trout!"

We rapidly snapped off some nearby thin branches and dashed back to the beck, puffing and panting as we did so. I don't know about the others, but the adrenaline was pumping through my system! Our 'dam' was about a foot high; we had the sticks and awaited our 'leader's' next order.

"Swizzle sticks int' watter ter make sure 'e stays over 'ere!"

As we 'swizzled' Tom lay full length on the large stone and gently placed his hand into the water and underneath the stone. The trout shot out like a rocket towards our 'swizzling' sticks and in a flash returned to its refuge!

"Cor it's a big un" I said, "about fifteen inches long!"

Once again our 'leader' carefully placed his hand into the water and underneath the stone. There was a flash as the trout streaked across the pool avoiding our 'swizzling' sticks and disappeared underneath another large stone on our side of the beck. As we knelt down and tried to peer underneath the stone there was another order.

"Try an' grab t'bugger!"

Following our 'leader's orders and example, I removed my jacket, rolled up my right shirt sleeve, then slowly put my hand into the very cold water. There was a shout from the opposite side of the beck.

"Move yer 'and very slowly to an' fro until yer can feel t'trout. Use thee middle finger ter tickle 'is belly!"

Being stretched out full length on this large stone with my head hanging down close to the water was not the best position to either nod my head or shout. Very carefully and slowly, with my middle finger extended, I placed my whole forearm deeper into the icy cold water and underneath the stone. Clinging to this large stone for support, with my hair touching the water, I slowly moved my hand to and fro. At first all I could feel was the icy cold water, then suddenly my middle finger touched the trout, which, as before, shot across the pool to its original refuge. I knelt on the stone and pointed.

"Theer, theer!

That was it! Our 'leader' removed his clogs and socks and jumped into the pool! Recalling his original 'orders' about being careful, there was no finesse. Grabbing wildly underneath the stone, the battle now commenced in earnest! Up to his knees in water and ignoring the splashes onto his clothing, wherever the trout went he pursued it! What with the noise of the 'beck', plus the numerous splashing and shouts made by our 'leader' of

"Missed t'buggger!"

He, by this time, was soaking wet, with the scene illuminated by the afternoon sunlight filtering through the trees, it was a sight to behold! Twice the trout almost escaped from the pool but was deterred by our 'swizzling' sticks. The trout's frenzy to escape was matched by our 'leader's' determination that it wouldn't! As it sped from one refuge to another it was pursued! Then it made a fatal mistake. Perhaps from exhaustion, it paused just for a fraction of a second in the shallowest part of the pool. Our 'leader' struck! Flinging himself onto the trout, for a few seconds his hands made contact! Would the trout escape yet again? He made another grab! This time flinging himself full length onto the trout! He grabbed again underneath his body, and then with a yell of triumph, he stood up and, with great difficulty clung on to his threshing catch! Dripping wet he 'sloshed' his way to the bank.

"Quick give us a stick ter 'donk 'im'!"

It was a beautiful brown trout three inches shorter than my original estimate. It was 'donked' on the head – it quivered and its threshing tail went still. Our 'leader' was grinning 'from ear to ear'!

"I said it were a big bugger. Me mumm'll be pleased an' we'll 'ave it fur us teas."

With these words we three realised that any ideas we may have had about cooking the trout beside the beck and sharing in its consumption was not to be. It was time to head for home.

On the way we talked about the trout and how it nearly escaped, adding words of praise about our 'leader's' efforts.

Arriving at our front door, as I pushed it open Nellie called from the kitchen.

"Is that you Alastair?"

"Aye Nellie, it's me."

"Did yer catch owt?"

Her head appeared around the kitchen door.

"Aye, it were a big 'un and Tom took it home fur his mumm."

"Our Jack'll be in soon and Harold is with his rabbits. Kettle's almost boiling, so go and wash yer hands."

The reader may have noticed that I had adopted the familys' normal response when the front door was opened. For example,

"Is that you Jack? Aye mumm it's me."

Although I had developed a Yorkshire accent, I had done so but without dropping my aitches. Somehow it didn't seem 'reet' ter do so.

Some weeks later we four were again lured on by the thought of taking home a big fat trout. On route we visited the first reservoir. As before there were dozens of large trout swimming lazily around and, from time to time, rising to the surface to snatch some insect that had landed on the water. The resultant ripples flashing like liquid gold as they spread across the surface and continued to increase in size. We realised that our previous efforts had failed, so we continued up the hill.

At the second reservoir we paused and stood very close to the edge. Peering into the water, there were the trout about fifteen inches below the surface. To catch even one we would be faced with exactly the same problem as before. For some minutes we sat watching these large trout. Tom seemed to know all about trout. He pointed.

"Them trout's brown, tuther kind 's rainbows, but yer don't git 'em 'ere."

We continued to sit by the edge of the reservoir wondering what to do. We were about a mile from the village and it was far too early to return home. Someone suggested going down to the beck again.

"Theer's trout in theer. If we catch wun we can cook it."

As we didn't have any matches this idea failed to inspire. Then Tom said,

"Let's try t'reservoir reet at t'top."

It seemed a good idea and it was somewhere that I had not visited during my previous Saturday rambles. We continued up the hill until we reached the top reservoir. Unlike the other two there were hardly any trees. As we walked up to the edge, unlike the other two reservoirs, this one was very much deeper, the water being held back by a series of stone ledges going deeper and deeper until they disappeared from sight. I peered into the water. There wasn't a sign of a trout. We walked along the bank. All I could see were these stone ledges disappearing into the depths. It was a very warm day and we were hot from our exertions. It seemed opportune to sit beside the water and eat our sandwiches, and drink the large bottle of 'Dandelion and Burdock' which we had purchased with our pooled resources. Despite the cool breeze blowing across the reservoir I was hot and sweaty. Having removed my jacket I sat by the edge, eating my sandwiches and with my companions, taking it in turns to have several 'swigs' of 'Dandelion and Burdock'. To reduce our over-heated condition we now removed our shirts and vests, enjoying the wafting of the cool breeze on our bare tops, plus the warmth of the afternoon sunshine.

After a while, someone said, "Me feet's 'ot so I'm gayin ter stick 'em int' watter."

As this seemed to be an excellent idea, off came our clogs and socks. The water was icy cold! Like the others I paddled and splashed my feet, enjoying the sensation.

Young boys can be very foolish. It started by our 'trout expert' saying, "I bet nobody dares ter jump int' watter."

Being young, and very foolish, I rose to the challenge. After all I came from Brighton! I recalled my mother taking me to the sea-front, usually early in the morning, and together we would wade up to our knees in the very cold sea-water before having the courage to dip down up to our chins. Armed with this knowledge I quickly removed my shorts and, wearing just my under-pants, jumped in! There was one fact that I had over-looked – I couldn't swim! The icy cold water took my breath away and I can recall seeing the light on the surface of the water. I was now in trouble! I managed to keep my eyes open and with my fingers coming into contact with the very slippery surface of the stone ledges, I clawed my way to the surface, and immediately went under again. At this stage I realised the seriousness of my situation! Throughout my struggles to survive I had kept my eyes open and the water was 'crystal clear'. What saved me was the construction of the reservoir. Had it not been for those stone ledges I would not be typing these words today. Despite the ledges being very slippery, I managed to use them to reach the surface and very close to the edge. I broke the surface gasping for breath as my three worried-looking companions grabbed me and pulled me out onto the bank. Despite the hot sun I was shivering, no doubt due to the combination of cold and shock. Tom's next statement was very much to the point.

"Yer daft buggger, yer very nearly drowned!"

I had been extremely foolish and it had been 'a very close call'. My other two friends
echoed Tom's sentiments.

"Bluddy 'ell Alastair, we thawt yer'd 'ad it!"

Having wrung out my under-pants and dressed, we were a very subdued group of boys as we made our way back down the hill towards the village. My thoughts were interrupted from time to time by my companions' comments describing in graphic detail my experience, some of which hurt my pride.

"I thawt anywun who lived by t'sea could swim."

I realised just how stupid I had been and I had to admit I had been very scared – but my main worry was how was I going to explain to Nellie my wet underpants?

13.   Wakes Week and meat pies with gravy

There was something entirely new in my experience – 'Wakes Week'. All the woollen mills closed down for a week's holiday and the impact on me was the very exciting prospect of being taken to the 'Wakes Week' fair at Keighley! My excitement mounted when Harold explained about the swings, the rounda- bouts, coconut shies, the lights, the music and the steam engines.

"As we git off t'bus yer'll 'ear t'music, not loud like, but yer'll 'ear it. Then yer'll see t'lights of them 'merry-go-rounds' an' the 'orses gayan upp an' down. Theer's great big steam engines, swings, 'urdy-gurdys' making lots of noisy music, coconut shies...."

The list if attractions seemed endless. I could hardly wait! However, Harold failed to mention that due to the war there would not be any coconut shies.

Faced with this huge list of attractions I commenced to save my 'choir-money', plus my weekly pocket-money that I received from Nellie for collecting the eggs and helping Harold with the rabbits and the chickens. A week before our visit to Keighley I had managed to put together almost two shillings and I had yet to receive my pocket-money! Not only was it important to be 'rich', it was also important to wear ones 'best' clothes. Some weeks before, I had been measured by Nellie and I was now the owner of a blue-serge jacket and shorts, plus a pair of grey-woollen knee-length stockings. Nellie thought that I looked "Reet smart." This suit was only ever worn on Sundays.

Everyone had a 'posh' set of clothes which were known as one's 'Sunday best' and as our visit to Keighley was special, I would be allowed to wear my recently acquired blue-serge suit. At school the constant question was,

"Are thee gayan ter t'fair?"

The 'big day' duly arrived. Dressed in my 'Sunday best', with Nellie and Harold similarly attired, Harold appeared downstairs sporting a new flat cloth cap, a starched collar and tie. Prior to our departure, Harold and I were inspected and any specs of dust were quickly removed by Nellie wielding a large clothes-brush. Having checked herself in the mirror above the fireplace and adjusted her hat, we were ready to make our way to the bus-stop. As we walked down the hill, passing the now silent mill on our right, I felt very special. It wasn't Sunday and I had my 'best suit' on, Harold and Nellie looked very smart and the night before Harold had polished our shoes, saying,

"Yer can't beat a reet good spit n'polish."

We boarded the bus and for a special treat we travelled on the 'top deck' so that I could see "Wot's wot." The bus-conductress pressed the bell twice and we set off for Keighley. On route Harold pointed out various things of interest, informing me,

"Me work's in Keighley, so I do this trip every day except Sundays."

Evidently Harold and Jack worked at the iron foundries in the town.

I had been to Keighley before on the choir-boys' day out. To my eyes it was full of grey stone buildings that looked as if they could do with a wash. As we alighted from the bus, we joined the crowds flocking to the fair. Everyone seemed happy and carefree. The first thing that I heard was the music! Even at a distance of several hundred yards, it was just as Harold had described it. There was a cacophony of sound as several dozen different tunes competed for attention. Then, as we drew near the numerous electric lights, I could see the 'merry-go-rounds' and the rising and falling wooden horses painted white and gold! We entered what normally must have been a park. Everywhere I looked were booths, some round, and some square, with red and white awnings, the interiors illuminated by bright electric lights. Harold pointed out the large steam engines. All the brass-work shone in the afternoon sun, their black painted exteriors covered in multi-coloured patterns and their tall chimneys emitting plumes of smoke.

"See them big engines over theer, when I were a lad they 'ad 'em ont' roads."

Harold pointed.

"Now that thing reet over theer is makin electricity fur t'lights."

I was holding Nellie's hand. She looked down at me through her thick-lensed glasses.

"Now, yer not ter go off on yer own. Yer've got ter stay with me and Harold."

There were so many exciting things to do and see and I was dying to spend some money and win a prize. With my 'choir money', plus pocket-money from Nellie, I had at least two shillings and four-pence. As most attractions cost a penny, with twenty-eight 'goes' I must win something! Harold looked down at me.

"Now what dus thar fancy? Theer's rolling t'penny, a ride on them 'orses over theer, or 'oop-la?"

"May I have a go at rolling t' penny? Then if I'm lucky I'll have more money fur the other things?"

We walked over to the booth. Harold explained what I had to do.

"Thar puts the penny intert slot on this wooden thing 'ere."

Harold demonstrated by placing my penny into the vertical slot.

"Now, thar keeps thar finger on't penny ter prevent it rolling away like. Cum 'ere and don't forget, keep thar finger on't penny."

Harold now directed my attention to the oil-skin cloth spread out before us.

"Now see all them squares? Each wun 'as a nummber. What thar has ter do is let go of t'penny an' try ter get it inter wun of them squares. So, if it lands on that ten over theer, thar gets ten pence back, plus yer own penny."

In my innocence this seemed to be 'money for old rope'. Now came my final instruction.

"Thar can direct this wooden slot thing in any direction. See where big nummbers are an' then tak the finger off t'penny."

I studied the numbered squares spread before me. One in the centre was marked five shillings! I carefully aimed the wooden guide containing one twenty-eighth of my 'wealth' – and lifted my finger. The penny rolled down the slot, held a straight course for about six inches, before veering off to one side and coming to rest with one of its edges outside a square marked with a 'one'. The booth owner, using what in essence was a small wooden rake, pulled my penny towards him and popped it into a large leather, open-necked bag, attached to his waist by a wide leather belt. I felt into the pocket of my navy blue shorts and withdrew another penny. I looked at the table again. The square marked five shillings had an allure that I could not resist. I placed the penny into the slot and once again carefully aimed to the right of the five shilling square, then lifted my finger. The penny rolled down the slot and on to the table, before again veering off to one side with its edge resting just outside a square marked with a four. As before, my penny disappeared into the capacious leather pouch. I looked up at Harold.

"It's not very easy."

Harold smiled.

"This time place thee penny 'arf way down t'slot."

I did as directed. This time the penny went about five inches before veering off to one side, where it wobbled before settling into a square marked with a 'one'! The owner of the booth briefly studied the position of the coin, then handed me back my penny plus one more! At last I knew how to win!

"Harold, Harold it worked!"

I was now 'on the road to riches'! Four pennies later I left the booth somewhat wiser with one seventh of my 'wealth' in the booth owner's pouch.

Nellie had been standing nearby speaking to another lady and now joined us.

"Well Alastair, how did yer do?"

I looked up at Harold.

"We did win wunce, didn't we Harold, butt in' end I lost four pence."

Nellie made a "tch" sound.

"Them booths are real 'catch pennies'."

She turned to Harold.

"Fancy takin t'lad to a booth like that!"

It had been my choice.

"Nellie I wanted to have a go, didn't I Harold?"

Harold ruffled my hair.

"That yer did and it wer funn. Now 'ow about a special treat? An ice-cream?"

I hadn't seen an ice-cream since leaving Brighton!

"Yes please. Can I have a cornet?"

"Of course yer can." He pointed. "It's just over theer."

Within minutes Harold returned holding three ice-cream cornets and handed one to me.

Clutching my cornet I took my first lick of a wartime ice-cream. It was very watery, quite yellow when compared to the ice-cream sold by 'Fortes' in Brighton, but to a small boy such differences were soon forgotten. As we walked around the fairground Harold tapped me on the shoulder.

"There's more booths 'ere' than yer can shake a stick at. Do they 'ave fairs like this in Brighton?"

I shook my head.

"Nay, theer's nowt like this."

There were lights, 'merry-go-rounds' with the white and gilded horses rising and falling in time to the music. There were large music-making machines producing what I can only describe as 'tinny' pipe music, and nearby were what Harold called 'boat swings'.

He pointed again.

"See them two ropes 'anging down? Yer sits in either end and tak it in turn ter pull on each rope. Watch them two lads theer."

The two boys, aged about fourteen, sat opposite to each other and pulled with gusto! The boat-swing started to oscillate backwards and forwards, rising higher and higher. I was keen to try it.

"Harold, can we have a go?"

Nellie interrupted.

"Alastair, not before yer've finished yer ice-cream, or it'll be all down t'front of yer new suit."

My new suit had been carefully chosen and purchased by Nellie. I wasn't involved in the choice, but I had to admit I did like the dark navy blue colour. When I had mentioned that the sleeves were too long, Nellie had replied:

"In three munths time it'll fit yer like a glove."

Despite Nellie's predictions, there was less than four weeks to go and the sleeves were still too long and just about touched my knuckles.

Harold turned to Nellie.

"'Ow about me an' thee an' lad 'aving a go?"

Nellie's response was not unexpected.

I'll watch, you go with Alastair."

Harold and I clambered aboard the boat-swing then sat down at each end. Harold leaned forward.

"Put yer feet against that board ont' floor and grab this 'ere rope."

I did so, but with my feet touching the foot-board my back was no longer in contact with the seat! Harold gave me a huge grin.

"Are yer ready? Pull!"

I did so and the swing moved about an inch. Harold shook his head.

"Nay, pull like this."

Harold pulled on his rope and my end started to rise into the air. Harold shouted:

"Now pull!"

I did so, but without my back being in contact with the seat my puny effort had little effect. However, thanks to gravity and Harold's pulling power, the swing rose higher and higher. At this stage self-preservation was more important! I clung to the sides of the swing, my feet pressed hard against the foot-board. With my shoulders only just in contact with the seat back the swing rose higher and higher! By the grin on his face Harold was obviously enjoying himself! Whilst I was thrilled I was not secure in the seat! As a result I was clinging onto the sides of the swing and I felt slightly scared. The swing's owner indicated that it was time to stop. Harold let go of his rope and the oscillations became smaller and smaller. The man in charge grabbed the side of the swing. We had stopped. Harold leaned forward.

"Well lad 'ow was that?"

"Just wonderful Harold, thank you very much."

I had to admit I was glad the swing had stopped. Harold helped me to the ground and scanned the attractions as he was keen to try another boat-swing. He pointed.

There's anuther over theer."

Nellie looked down at me.

"Well, did yer like that?"

"Yes Nellie, it was wonderful!"

We didn't visit the other boat-swing, but continued to wander around the fairground looking at all the different booths and attractions. There was a carnival atmosphere, people looked happy; teenage boys walked around holding their girlfriends' hands; the booths; the merry-go-rounds full of people; the music blaring out from various attractions; the numerous electric lights; the shouts of the booth owners trying to tempt people to try their luck. To my ears it was just a cacophony, a mixture of music from various pipe-organs, and noise that was almost overwhelming. In this heady mixture it was difficult to remember there was a war going on. The large crowd was out to have a good time!

We must have been wandering around for at least ten minutes. Harold turned to Nellie and jerked his thumb at the beer-tent.

"I'll just nip over theer."

Nellie's not unexpected response

"I've seen yer nips before. Stick ter wun pint, we'll be over by that 'helter-skelter over theer, and don't be long, we're off ter me Mum and Dad's fer tea."

Some twenty minutes later Harold appeared from out of the crowd looking highly pleased with himself.

"That wus jusst a quick wun."

Nellie retorted:

"That makes a change! We'd best be off."

Nellie's mother and father lived in a neat Victorian-type terraced house. To me they were very old and had kindly welcoming faces. I was introduced by Nellie.

"This is Alastair, all the way from Brighton and now he's wun of the family."

Granddad shook my hand.

"Have yer bin ter t'fair, a lad like you must want his tea."

We all sat around a table and I noted that it had very small patterns all over it. The predominant colour was dark red. This was now covered with a white table-cloth.

Tea consisted of tea-cakes (the usual large flat currant buns), potted meat and bread with home-made jam. The conversation was about Jack, other members of the family, and finally the fair. Granddad turned to me.

"Do yer have 'Wakes Week' in Brighton?"

"No Sir, but I always enjoy the summer holidays."

Granddad smiled.

"Bye, I've never bin called 'Sir' before. Yer musst call me Granddad."

Nellie leaned forward.

"Alastair's very polite."

And Harold added,

"'E's a bit of a boxer."

Granddad looked down at me and smiled.

"A boxer! After tea me and thee we'll have a spar."

With the tea things cleared and the white table-cloth carefully removed and folded, the red coloured cloth was smoothed. Granddad looked at me.

"Reet, let's have a go!"

He knelt down on the floor and held up his fists.

"Now yung Alastair, yer do t'same. Now what is the first thing yer do?"

I used the Yorkshire expression.

"Thummp him!"

Granddad smiled and shook his head.

"Yer watch their eyes and their fists. Now what do yer do?"

I shrugged my shoulders. Granddad continued,

"Keep yer distance until yer ready ter thummp him. Now let's have a go!"

He playfully leaned forward and poked me in the stomach.

"Now, yer weren't watching me eyes and me left fist."

He now went to poke me with his right fist and I stepped back.

"That's better, butt don't drop yer guard and choose yer moment ter thummp me."

I recalled the bloody nose I had given to Jack's friend.

"I don't want to hurt you."

Granddad laughed.

"Hurt me!"

He went to poke me in the ribs again. I stood back and timidly aimed a punch at his head. He swayed to one side so I missed.

"Yer need ter hit harder than that!"

Grandma intervened.

"That's enuugh! "

Granddad stood up and ruffled my hair.

"Next time yer cum, we'll have anuther 'boxing match'."

They were a kindly couple and I always enjoyed visiting them. True to his word, Granddad and I always had a 'boxing match'.

'Wakes Week' had almost faded from my memory. As a choirboy I had rehearsed for the forthcoming 'Harvest Festival'. The most favourite hymn was my favourite, 'We Plough the Fields and Scatter the Good Seed on the Land'. The church would be filled with flowers; russet apples; pears and root vegetables that had been scrubbed clean. There would be piles of cabbages; early Brussels-sprouts; sacks of well-scrubbed potatoes; trays of eggs and golden-brown bread shaped like sheaves of corn. To add to the atmosphere, there would be numerous flickering candles placed in prominent places. And so the day arrived! The choir and the congregation sang each hymn with gusto! The Vicar gave his usual long sermon on the 'Lord's bountiful gifts'. Following the service, as before, the choir was despatched to various needy folk with parcels of foodstuffs which had been donated from the local parishioners.

The Harvest Festival heralded the arrival of the first frosts. In the school playground the children would use the frost encrusted tarmac to make a slide. The first child would make perhaps no more than two to three feet and as each subsequent child added to this; the slide would be extended until it was at least ten yards long. The more it was used the better it became. A few of the girls joined in, but their favourite games, despite the frost, were still skipping and playing 'hopscotch'. As you will realise, early morning frosts meant wrapping up in warm clothing. Having said this, all the boys continued to wear shorts and stockings that only reached to just below the knees. Using a Yorkshire expression, "It made it reet parky!"

As the temperature continued to fall, Nellie provided me with a knitted khaki 'balaclava' that covered my entire head, ears and neck, leaving just my eyes and nose exposed to the elements. Any refusal to wear it evaporated with her well-chosen words.

"It's jusst like them soldiers wear."

With my "balaclava' tucked into my top-coat, a woollen scarf and gloves, plus a pair of clogs that I had to admit, although difficult to walk in, were warmer than my normal shoes, my body stayed warm but an icy wind blowing onto my knees and up the legs of my shorts ensured that my nether regions did not share the same level of comfort.

My 'Sunday best' was worn when attending church. My winter garb was superimposed with some minor changes. My 'balaclava' remained and I was provided with a small comb to tidy my hair before the Service. My Canadian sheepskin-lined jacket with its deep fur collar was imperative, and black shoes replaced my clogs.

My nether regions were still subjected to the icy cold air.

Winter meant ice crystals forming on the inside of my bedroom window. The solitary coal fire provided the hot water that was only tepid by morning. By leaving all the doors open, the same coal-fire kept the house warm. Winter meant that within an hour or so of leaving school, darkness descended on the village, the 'black-out' regulations making the darkness even more intense. Winter also meant hot meat pies every Saturday! Armed with a pint jug for the gravy and some coinage for the pies, I would set off down the hill.

During the winter the local pie shop enjoyed increased trade. I would queue outside with other children, plus a smattering of mothers, each of us clutching the obligatory jug to carry the steaming hot gravy. The pies were served hot, so clutching the paper bag with one's free hand and with the fingers of the other hand resting lightly against the side of the jug, ensured arriving home without numb fingers. The pies were dome-shaped, about four inches in diameter, a deep golden brown colour and contained a mixture of a minuscule amount of meat, plenty of potato, and were very tasty. It was an errand that I always enjoyed as the aroma wafting from the pie shop immediately converted me into a copy of the famous 'Bisto Kids'. Despite the passage of years, that wonderful aroma is seared into my memory.

The postman seldom called – the main post being letters from home. Whilst I missed my mother and her immediate family and enjoyed reading their letters, Nellie had to remind me from time to time saying,

"Yer haven't written to yer nuther recently!"

It was about this time that the postman called – the letter was addressed to Nellie. Arriving home from school at dinner time, Nellie told me that my mother was coming to visit me. It was tremendous news! Nellie re-read the letter.

"Yer muther says she hopes to be here on Saturday. She's cumming all the way from Brighton! Now what do yer think of that?"

The day of the visit drew closer. On Friday night I said my prayers and hopped into bed. Nellie came to say goodnight, switched off the light and as usual left the bedroom door open.

"Alastair, get a good neet's sleep, we don't want yer muther meeting a sleepy-eyed lad."

At first sleep eluded me. How long was it since I had seen my mother? My mind drifted back to the day I had left Brighton. Of our original class there were few of us left. I recalled how I had missed her and the family, but now I had been embraced by this very kind Yorkshire family. My main friends were not from my former classmates but boys from the village. I tossed and turned as these and many other thoughts, including Harold's rabbits went through my mind, until finally sleep closed my eyes.

I awoke to a very cold and frosty morning. Pulling back the curtains, the bottom of each windowpane had traces of frost. From downstairs I could hear movement and there was a smell of hot fat wafting up the stairs. Then I heard Nellie's voice.

"Alastair, are yer awake? Don't forget, yer muther's cuming."

I walked to the top of the stairs.

"Aye Nellie, I'm awake. I'll have a wash and cum down."

"Don't be long breakfast'll be ont' table soon."

As it was Saturday it was hot pie day. Just before mid-day I set off down the hill with my jug and sufficient money to purchase one extra pie. As it was Winter I was dressed in my usual garb including my clogs and 'balaclava'. Having queued, I emerged from the shop with a paper bag containing five hot pies and a jug of steaming hot gravy and set off for home. Suddenly I saw my mother coming towards me! I can still recall the shocked look on her face as I greeted her with a very broad Yorkshire accent! We hugged each other as the tears trickled down our faces. She was just as pretty as I had remembered her. We walked back up the hill hand in hand. I held the jug and my mother held the bag of hot pies. Little did I realise that this was the last time I would walk up this hill. That afternoon, despite any bombing, I was on my way back to Brighton!

It had been a series of rapid and tearful goodbyes. I hugged Nellie, Harold and Jack. It had all been so sudden! I hugged them all again and the tears continued to flow. As my mother and I walked down the hill carrying my few possessions, I did so with 'a 'lump in my throat'. I was leaving a family that I had grown to love. I now had my mother and I would soon be back with the other members of my family. The feelings that I had were not so dissimilar to those that I had experienced when I had last seen my mother waving to me as the coach departed from Ditchling Road School.

As we boarded the bus for Keighley, through the window I could see the church. As I did so I recalled my friends in the choir, the Harvest Festivals, Mid-night Mass and singing carols around the village and feeling the snow 'scrunching' beneath my feet. As the conductress pressed the bell, I realised that this was the end of my life in Yorkshire – and from now on all I would have would be memories.

Children have short memories and it was only in later years that I recalled this Yorkshire family who had made me feel so welcome, had cared for me and made me happy. I vowed to return to thank them for all their kindness. Then, due to the passage of years, it was too late. Even now as I write these words I deeply regret that I failed to make that journey to say just two words: *"Thank you"*.

14.   Home at last!

In the weeks and months that followed, I was ridiculed for my Yorkshire accent by both my cousins and the children of my former school. I no longer said "come", it was "cum." The word "yes" was now "aye", and my class-mates taunted me when I mentioned "me muther." To add insult to injury, after two weeks I was placed into the 'B' class as my Yorkshire education was below the 'A' standard that I had attained prior to my departure. On their return the other evacuee children would suffer in the same way. Shown a sentence I could not pick out the verb – and nouns and pronouns were beyond my comprehension. I can recall the teacher saying,

"Alastair, a verb is a 'doing word', it is an action word, and an adverb describes how it is being done."

She pointed to the word 'running'.

"This is an action word so it's the verb. The next word is the adverb 'quickly' which describes how the action is being carried out."

Despite this information I failed to see why giving words strange names was important.

You will have gathered that my home-coming was a mixture of joy and misery.

Sometimes I longed for our rambles on the Yorkshire moors and the boyhood country pursuits; collecting the eggs after school; helping Harold with his rabbits and chickens; being in the choir and the various church festivals.

My Yorkshire accent did not 'disappear over-night'. However, finally with the passage of time the taunting ceased when my southern accent replaced my previous dialect. As the final few evacuees returned, they also faced the same degree of ridicule and joined me in the 'B' stream.

The threat of invasion no longer existed, which no doubt partly influenced my mother to return me to Brighton. The war in the air continued at a less intensive pace. Sometimes during daylight hours the vapour trails of the enemy's and our own aircraft could be seen and heard due to the distant sound of machine-gun fire. Boys constantly arrived at school with spent cartridge cases to show admiring friends, or to use these as 'swops' for other items of discharged weaponry. Against this background, and having been absorbed into home and school, life returned to 'normal'. However, life can be full of surprises. Little did I realise that in the not too distant future the German air force would turn this situation 'onto its head'.

Under our roof there were now four people – my mother, grandmother, Aunt Hilda and myself. Aunt Hilda was still employed as an electrician's mate and from her, in addition to my standard 'pocket-money', I received two shillings and sixpence (12.5p) every week! As a result I was now 'rich'! This extra level of funds allowed me to purchase balsa-wood cut-outs of model aircraft to be trimmed and sanded to the correct profiles prior to painting and affixing the R.A.F roundels and squadron markings. My two favourite models were the Bolton-Paul 'Defiant'. This was an unusual aircraft. It was a fighter aircraft, but, in addition to the pilot it had a rear-gunner who was housed in a rotating turret that could engage enemy aircraft in a 180 degree arc. The other model was the 'Lysander'. It was a high-wing monoplane with a radial engine and was used to deliver equipment and secret agents into France. This was due to its short take-off and landing capability. With a sharp knife and sand-paper, I spent many happy hours fashioning these balsa wood shapes into miniature replicas of the real thing.

As far as the family was concerned the major change was that Uncle Bill, due to his age, had been discharged from the army and had returned to help build railway-engines. My cousin Vic had joined the 'Home Guard'. Uncle Bob was still in the R.A.F and looked very smart in his uniform. My mother had maintained sporadic contact with my father. I can recall when we lived in Polegate, their meetings had taken place in Eastbourne. The only impact on me at that time was he had purchased two presents to be delivered by my mother. The first was a number of 'Mickey Mouse' slides for my candle-powered 'magic-lantern', and a model of Sir Malcolm Campbell's world speed record breaking car, 'Bluebird'. From the 'snippets' of conversation between my mother and grandmother, it was evident that my mother 'was clutching at straws'.

I digress. Brighton was not a target, so apart from the air-battles over Sussex we could sleep soundly in our beds. One afternoon after school some very loud explosions were heard, followed in seconds by the roar of low flying aircraft. Evidently the viaduct that spanned the London Road had been the target. Steam locomotives were being built at Brighton; therefore by severing the rail-link out of Brighton it 'bottled-up' production. The bombs had fallen at least a mile or more away from our house, so we were not in any danger. However, at the time of the attack Aunt Lucy was shopping in the London Road and arrived at our house covered in dust and in a state of shock. Upon seeing my grandmother she hugged her and burst into-tears! This incident was to form the catalyst for not only my return to Yorkshire, but also our entire household!

With Aunt Lucy's 'near miss' but a few days old, I was aware that during the inevitable cups of tea, supported by my grandmother 'consulting the tea-leaves'. (At this stage tea-bags had yet to be invented), therefore when a cup of tea had been consumed, the used leaves residing in the base of each cup were closely scrutinised and the 'pictures' formed by the residual leaves were discussed in great detail. Normally it was my grandmother who pronounced her 'findings'. It must have been the 'pictures' formed by the used tea-leaves that produced the various 'messages'. By adding Aunt Lucy's 'near miss', this formed the basic 'reason' for our eventual departure. In later years I realised that logic, even in its most basic form, did not exist within our four walls. To this day I fail to understand why the family left the comfort of our home and opted to depart to Yorkshire. Apart from the aforementioned raid, Brighton was not being bombed and the threat of invasion no longer existed. I had settled back into my 'old' school and my Yorkshire accent no longer existed – so where was the logic for this totally unexpected move?

15.   The unexpected return to Yorkshire

Prior to our departure, Aunt Hilda had been despatched to Yorkshire with my grandmother's assurance that 'according to the leaves' she would find suitable accommodation. Within ten days her letter confirmed that she had been allocated a suitable house set aside for 'evacuee' families. If we had 'rose coloured spectacles' as the family read her letter about our 'new' home to be – these were to be dispelled even before we opened the front door.

Our departure for 'pastures new' was accompanied by numerous suitcases, two carrier -bags containing our rationed foods and a cabin-trunk, which evidently contained the family's' bedding. I have no idea what happened to our normal family goods and chattels, perhaps these were stored with the remaining members of grandmother's vast Victorian family. To continue: travelling by train with this mass of baggage was not without its difficulties. Petrol was rationed and only allocated to essential services, so taxis were almost non-existent. As a result with help from a sweating peroxide blonde conductress (peroxide was used by women to bleach their hair), plus the exertions of several elderly gentlemen passengers, (remember, most of the men were in the Forces), our baggage was loaded onto a bus, filling and over-spilling from the under-stairs luggage area and onto the rear seats. As my grandmother was fully convinced that 'thieves lurked around every corner', not one item of luggage left our sight for the entire journey.

By early evening we had again taken a bus from the nearest railway-station and we, plus our pile of luggage, had been deposited on the roadside. With no porters within five miles and no other willing hands, Aunt Hilda led the way and our baggage was 'leap-frogged' the four hundred or so yards to our 'new' abode.

The house was one of a small terrace, situated on a corner and faced onto an unpaved road and the canal. In the fading light to my eyes it looked grim from the outside. This pre-conditioning proved to be beneficial, as when we entered through the badly painted front door, the house smelt musty and was in semi-darkness. A coin inserted into the electric meter which was in the hallway illuminated our surroundings, and the same action to the gas meter, which was also in the hallway, proved that the ancient, blackened cooker was working.

Apart from what we had eaten on our journey we were almost devoid of food, except for the contents of our two carrier bags that contained our rationed foodstuffs. A kind neighbour had left a jug of milk (bottles did not exist in the village), together with a small note bidding us welcome. At least we could have a hot drink. A quick inspection revealed that the house was sparsely furnished. The hall led into a large kitchen, passing a stairway that led to the upstairs and three small bedrooms. The flush toilet was outside. The bath was a galvanised affair and was within the kitchen. It was covered with a series of wooden-planks that when horizontal provided an over large shelf, which could be lifted and secured to the wall when its galvanised 'companion' was in use. We also discovered that it had to be filled and emptied by hand. With its tiny lounge that faced directly onto the unpaved street, no garden whatsoever, plus the cream painted wooden boarding that covered the hallway and the stair-well and the toilet was outside, the overall picture that faced us matched out mood – utter despair. So much for tea-leaves!

16. Schooldays are the happiest – or are they?

You will recall that when I returned to Brighton from my original sojourn in Yorkshire, at school within two weeks I was relegated from Class 2a to Class 2b which was for the 'not so bright' pupils. My contribution to Class 2a had consisted of (a) A broad Yorkshire accent and (b) Very neat hand-writing. It was from this lowly category of Class 2b, this time with my mother, grandmother and Aunt Hilda, I returned to Yorkshire.

Within one day of our arrival my mother took me to the village school. From the front door we turned left passing Mrs. Oliver's shop. Our route followed the canal which was to our right – then along the unpaved road. At the hump-backed bridge we turned right, crossing the canal. Then we walked beside the church-yard and onto a road where we turned left passing the church on our left with the school being adjacent. The school was surrounded by railings (yet to be removed to assist the war effort). It had a tar macadam playground to its front and the actual entrance into this single storey building was accessed through a large porch. This led immediately into one of two classrooms. I was to discover that the entire school was divided into two classrooms. A lady teacher presided over the younger elements and the Headmaster over the remainder. However, I am jumping ahead.

The noise from the playground reached our ears just after crossing the small hump-backed bridge and reached a crescendo as we arrived outside the school entrance. As per my first day at my original Yorkshire school, I was dressed in school-uniform which consisted of; a grey jacket and shorts, a grey matching cap with a badge on the front; grey knee-length stockings with the turn over tops ringed in two dark red circles; a grey pullover; a red and black horizontally striped school tie; a white shirt; well polished black shoes, and in my right-hand trouser pocket the inevitable carefully ironed and folded white handkerchief. In contrast, most of my future classmates wore an assortment of clothing, ranging from the downright scruffy- and in some cases soiled clothing, and as you would expect, clogs. To say that I 'stood out like a sore thumb' was an understatement!

Our arrival caused a momentary lull in the playground's raucous activity – it appeared that every eye was upon us. We entered the wide porch to be met by the lady teacher who greeted us in a mild Yorkshire accent, and then went to find the Headmaster. He was of medium height and build, thinning grey hair, wore 'tortoise-shell' spectacles and was clean-shaven. He was dressed in a mid-grey suit; white shirt with a starched collar; a non-descript tie and highly polished brown brogue shoes. Apart from a beaming smile to my mother, I received a brief hand-shake and a fleeting smile.

My immediate impression was not one of a kind-hearted man. I can recall a strange feeling in my stomach, part of which no doubt, was caused by being thrust into this new environment. He informed me that I would be in his class. With my mother's departure the Headmaster took me into the second classroom. Ahead of us was a blackboard, some thirty old-looking wooden desks that could have been in service during Dickens time. In front of the blackboard was a slightly raised area, upon which and in the centre, was the Headmaster's desk. To the right of the raised area was a door that I was to discover led into a small store-room that contained a water-tap and a large ceramic 'butler's sink'. On that first day little did I realise that this room would feature in a major confrontation. The classroom had a high ceiling and was light and airy. The outside structure was (as stated) of grey stone and the building had a pitched slate-tiled roof. I was to learn that it was a Church of England school, which accounted for the frequent visits by the local Vicar.

With only two classrooms and two teachers the school was divided as follows. The lady teacher taught the junior pupils whose ages ranged from seven to nine, and the Headmaster taught the ten to fourteen year olds. The classes were uni-sex and sub-divided by year. No easy task to switch from one curriculum to the next.

On this first morning I stood in front of the class beside the Headmaster and I was introduced, the Headmaster making full use of the word "evacuee" which over- emphasised that I was different. However I thought that I was the sole curiosity, not only due to my dress but my recovered southern accent. Following my introduction I was allocated a desk near the front of the class and within the section of my peer group.

At break-time having consumed our free one-third pint of milk, we entered the playground. No one offered to fight me, I was accepted into the class and I commenced to answer their many questions about bombs and German aircraft. This was confined to the boys. The girls kept looking in my direction, and then going into a huddle, making shy glances. It was during this first break-time that I was approached by a boy of my age who, from his accent, now slightly tinged with the Yorkshire dialect, told me that he came from London and that he and his mother occupied an 'evacuee house' right beside the canal and next to the swing-bridge situated some one hundred yards from our 'new' abode. We were to become firm friends.

You may recall that when we left Brighton I had been in Class 2b which was for 'the not so bright' pupils. Within days of arriving at this new school there was a rapid reversal of role. I was deemed to be the 'bright boy' of my class. The reason was that the Brighton curriculum was in advance of this small Yorkshire village school. At the end of the school year I was awarded a prize in the form of a book for being top of my class. At the end of my complete school year I was awarded another book for being 'top of the school' across all subjects. However, this was in the future, the day-to-day running of this class was not all 'sweetness and light'. The reason? Here as in my previous Yorkshire school, corporal punishment was liberally applied and delivered in front of the class by the Headmaster using a leather strap onto the palm of an outstretched hand. This type of punishment was only given to the boys. To my mind this liberal use of the strap was in many cases totally unjustified. As before, seeing these acts of brutality always gave me an unpleasant feeling in the pit of my stomach. Ten lashings with the strap was commonplace. Initially, no doubt being the 'new-boy' and considered to be 'bright' I escaped this form of punishment. However, as I became adjusted to my environment and my southern accent absorbed the local dialect, I too would be ordered to stand in front of the class and hold out my left hand, palm uppermost. More on this subject later.

Arriving home after this first day at school I accompanied my mother shopping. On the end of our short terrace was a small sweet-shop run by a middle-aged lady called Mrs. Oliver. Apart from sweets and chocolate, (which were rationed), Mrs Oliver also stocked bread and other commodities. The main groceries came from the Co-op which was situated past the swing-bridge to our left, where my new friend lived, and some twenty-five yards ahead on our right in the High Street. Here were a number of small non-descript shops, including the inevitable clog shop and a barber. Further up the High Street was a butcher's shop. Our milk was delivered daily by the local farmer Chris Ager driving a two wheel horse-drawn cart, the milk being in large churns and dispensed with two metal dippers into jugs held up by the local housewives. The dippers were either a half-pint or one pint size and the dippers were constantly 'swizzled' around within the churns to keep the cream dispersed. It was at this farm that I was to spend many happy hours. However, during these early days this was an unknown experience. I digress.

At this juncture it is worth pausing to pass comment about the local barber. As before, in the first Yorkshire village only two styles existed. The first being 'short back and sides'. The hair on the sides of the head being reduced to skin length by vigorous application of hand held clippers, normally dug into the flesh. What was left on top of the head was rapidly reduced in length. A parting was the final act. The end result resembled an escapee from a public institution. This 'scalping' from memory cost sixpence: (two and a half pence in today's coinage). The other 'style' cost tuppence – i.e a third of a sixpence. You will recall this was called 'notching' and took about a third of the time of a 'normal' haircut. Again you will recall that a ceramic pudding basin was an essential piece of equipment. Any hair showing below its rim was 'reduced to skin length'. With the basin removed, any hair remaining was cut very short with scissors. Anyone undergoing this treatment resembled an escaped convict! Some of the very poor families could not afford the higher priced 'haircut'.

Let us now continue with a description of the High Street. Almost next to the Co-op was the social hall where dances were sometimes held and where the Boy Scouts and Girl Guides gave their concerts to doting parents and grandparents, aunts and uncles, who in some cases were oblivious to 'little Jimmy's', or 'little Mary's' off-key renderings. On the opposite side of the road, and before the butcher's shop, was the village church-hall where locally organised concerts were held under the benign eye of the Vicar where his 'flock' could expose their 'talents'. As a local cinema did not exist, and a bus-ride to the nearest town cost well in excess of being entertained at the village hall, it will come as no surprise that the concerts were always 'packed out'. So in essence this was our very small village shopping and recreation area with the addition of the church, the school, the farm and the surrounding countryside, this represented my 'new world'.

At school I soon made friends with Billy who also lived in the same road facing onto the canal and some twenty-five yards closer to the village shops. As he passed our door on his way to school he called on a regular basis and we made our way to school together, crossing the small humped-backed bridge that I had crossed with my mother on my first day. Also taking the same route were two girls who were in our class, Betty and Monica. They were very pretty and very interested in stories about bombs and German aeroplanes. Most days they walked to school with us. Some time later I was invited to join with them, plus several other boys and girls from my class, in various activities that were normally confined to early evenings and week-ends.

In these days of plenty it seems incredible that very poor people existed during the nineteen-forties. One of the boys in our class always appeared wearing ragged clothes. From his obvious body-odour, notched' hair-cut, dirty face and unpolished clogs, plus his sad face, he looked poor and obviously was poor. He was often the butt of the more 'wealthy' pupils. This was not helped by the Headmaster constantly bringing him to the front of the class, pointing out his unkempt condition. I had no idea where he lived, or his circumstances, but from his appearance the house must have been filthy. This poor boy was often the victim of the Headmaster's strap. I cannot recall his 'misdemeanours', but to my mind he was constantly singled out for unjustified punishment.

The Headmaster was a very good artist and it was from him that my artistic flair developed. Being in the heart of the Yorkshire countryside we had ample subjects on which to lavish paint onto paper. In the spring and summer there was an abundance of wild flowers. In the autumn dried leaves still attached to their twigs. With winter it was holly and still life, the objects ranging from a single book (this gave us an insight into perspective), to one of the Headmaster's highly polished shoes (the polished surface teaching us light and shade). When using water-colour we were only provided with the basic colours – red, dark blue, yellow and black. From these we produced the many and varied colours as depicted by our various subjects. Apart from the paints we were provided with two brushes, one fine and the other medium and also a small cloth that was used to wipe the colour from the brushes and washed out after each painting session. Finally a very small amount of water, normally contained in a discarded 'Shippams' paste jar, which was some three and a half inches in height, bulbous in shape and some two inches in diameter. Prior to rationing the 'Shippams' Company produced various edible pastes ranging from pilchard and salmon, to a range of meats. These were widely used by the buying public. Being so small you will realise that they contained very little water. These tiny jars of water held a very significant place in each art lesson – the water had to remain almost clear. To anyone accustomed to 'swizzling' a brush full of colour into these pristine jars was the 'ultimate sin' and for the boys resulted in the strap. How was it possible to paint in various colours and use this minuscule amount of water and only tinge it? The answer was the small piece of cloth. This was constantly used to wipe the brushes from the base of the hairs to the tip, then, and only then, dipping only the tip of the brush into the water and again wiping the brush. This lesson has remained with me to this day.

It was 'under the eye' of the Headmaster that my latent talents started to emerge, which culminated some year or so later when I was selected to attend the Leeds Art College. This was after passing my 'eleven-plus' examination. It never came to pass as the family returned to Brighton, where my artistic 'talents', plus a broad Yorkshire accent and a curriculum below par resulted yet again in my being categorised as not very 'bright' and I was not going to Grammar School.

Being, in the eyes of the village Headmaster, 'talented', as far as art was concerned, ensured that I received special attention. Even now, thinking back to those formative days and some seventy plus years later, there is no doubt in my mind that it was this Headmaster who encouraged me to observe objects and people with a 'very keen eye'. One of his 'tricks' was, when observing a subject, to view it with almost closed eyes. The effect is to heighten the areas of light and shade. If you doubt this, may I suggest that you try it?

From the above a picture may be emerging of a kindly middle-aged man bringing out the various and varied talents of his pupils. Do not overlook the liberal use of the strap. I had been at the school for some months when for some very minor 'offence' (which normally at Ditchling Road School would have resulted in detention), I was ordered to stand in front of the class with my left arm outstretched and palm uppermost to receive five lashings of the strap. The first one hurt like hell and this level of pain increased with the other four. The pain was intense and caused the palm of my left hand to swell and turn red. I returned to my desk trying not to show the pain – after all boys do not cry and certainly not in front of girls.

Some months later again I was ordered to come forward to receive the strap. With the passage of time I cannot remember the reason, but to my mind it was totally unjustified. When walking forward with a very dry mouth and my heart thudding in my chest I decided that I would not succumb. I was ordered to hold out my left hand and I refused. The whole class stared in utter disbelief! You could have 'heard a pin drop'. The Headmaster with strap in hand again ordered me to hold out my hand. Again I refused, saying (with a very dry mouth) his proposed use of the strap was totally unjustified. He went very red in the face and I was ordered to enter the small store-room that was to the right of the blackboard. I was trembling as I opened the door and had visions of being flogged. What could I do? In the ceramic 'butlers sink' was a white enamel jug. I quickly filled this with water as with strap in hand and with the same red face the Headmaster arrived. No doubt he quickly deduced my intentions. I could see from his face that he was furious! His voice was full of menace.

"Put that jug down!"

I was trembling with fear and I held the jug in front of me with both hands. My mouth was so dry it was difficult to speak.

"Take one step towards me and I'll throw this water all over you!"

Would he lash out with the strap? Despite being frightened I fully intended to carry out my threat. He hesitated.

"For the last time, put that jug down!"

My response was an emphatic "No!" I could see he too was shaking, no doubt with rage and frustration. Perhaps it was the thought of reappearing before the class with his suit front soaked with water that 'won the day'. He put the strap down.

"I promise not to hit you, although for threatening me you deserve it. Go back to your desk."

I did not feel any form of triumph, I had a horrible feeling in the pit of my stomach realising that perhaps this was not the final outcome of my proposed threat. All I had done was to avoid an unjustified beating. As I re-entered the classroom all whispering stopped and all eyes were upon me. I sat down. I still had a dry mouth and could not hide my shaking hands. Billy looked at me and shrugged his shoulders and 'pulled a face in a questioning manner. My only response was a slight shake of the head. The Headmaster resumed his place at his desk. What would he say? He looked around the class and then at me. He pointed.

"I do not wish to say what this boy has done. Let it suffice to be said it was very serious."

He scanned the class again.

"It could result in his being expelled from this school."

There was a gasp from the class! The pupils seated in front of me all turned around and looked at me. He continued to talk about discipline. His previous statement about being expelled filled me with horror! Expelled! It had never entered my head that this could be the final outcome. My hands continued to shake. Having completed his statement to the class we were given a brief break. In the playground I was besieged by both boys and girls asking me what had happened? I did not wish to elaborate and simply said that I had not received the strap. On the way home that afternoon I told Billy the whole story. He grinned.

"Yer should 'ave drowned t'old bugger!"

Following this incident I remained at the school and never again did I receive the strap. I also had the impression that the Headmaster's liberal use of the strap had been partially curtailed, or is it with the passage of time my feelings are now more benign?

Arriving at home that day I was in a quandary. Should I tell my mother? The Headmaster had mentioned my possible expulsion from the school. I agonised over what I should do. Finally I decided to say nothing, the main reason being, that if my mother agreed that my action had been justified, I had little doubt she would visit the school and confront the Headmaster. Within a few days I ceased agonising as other out-of-school activities took 'pride of place'.

Before continuing I wish to digress onto a subject with medical overtones: boils. As per the previous village, folklore existed amongst the boys and youths regarding how to treat boils; a subject that was not normally discussed in polite society. It was some weeks soon after commencing at this 'new' school that I became aware of the existence, yet again, of boils. As before this painful condition was for some unknown reason suffered only by boys and callow youths. Again, as before, I first became aware of this condition when a boy within my class was seen to be apparently suffering from a stiff neck. On closer inspection it revealed a large pink elasticated plaster affixed just above and to the right of his collarless shirt. I knew that boils "Urt like 'ell!" Some week later I noted another boy with a plaster also on his neck. This time the plaster had a small hole in its centre "Ter git t'puss out." If the reader is, as before feeling squeamish I am not surprised. Remember, worse is to follow! The reason for this are the three methods employed to 'cure' this painful condition. There were the fervent supporters: the 'squeezers'. Wait until the boil is 'ripe'. Next there were the 'hot bottlers'. You will recall that a beer or lemonade bottle was carefully filled with very hot water, then emptied and placed over the boil. As the bottle cools it sucks. Ugh!

The third was to lance the boil with a razor blade.

I am more than thankful that during my time in the village boils and I stayed away from each other. What was the cause? I have no idea; maybe the water? Or was it a poor diet? Whenever I think about my time within these two villages, boils always feature in my recollections.

17.   To be a farmer's boy

A road ran in front of the school and then headed towards the canal where it was crossed by a wooden hand-operated swing bridge. The road then continued up the hill passing a large grassy field to its left. Finally arriving at a 'T' Junction one turned left and within less than fifty yards was a farm. It was from this farm that our morning milk was delivered by the farmer driving a two wheeled horse drawn cart containing metal churns of milk. I seem to recall it was one Saturday when I stood with jug in hand outside our front-door awaiting to receive and pay for our two dippers (two pints) of milk. The farmer was a bluff red faced kindly man, slightly rotund, who always wore a flat cap and a brown three-quarter length jacket. Attached by a leather cross-strap was a leather satchel into which he placed the 'milk money' and issued change. He was well liked and always had a ready smile. Having filled my jug he said:

"Does thar want a job?"

Work had never entered my head. He continued:

"Cows need mucking out, then in't summer theers hay-making. Pay's not bad, a shilling a week. What does thar think?"

With hindsight he was just being kind and perhaps felt sorry for our family's situation. So I took the job on the princely pay of (as agreed) one shiny silver shilling per week. Added to my weekly 'pocket-money' of sixpence – I was now 'rich'! To use the word 'job' is a misnomer as I am sure my puny efforts must have had a minuscule effect on the day-to-day running of the farm. But whatever I did was enjoyable and I was soon joined by the other evacuee boy who was from London. Between us, we helped muck-out the cows and herd them in and out of the milking shed to be rewarded from time to time with a dipper of cream that was no doubt used to serve the following day's milk. Another of our tasks was to search the hedgerows for eggs deposited by hens who for some unknown reason were reluctant to use the hen-house.

It was also during late spring and early summer that we roamed the large field below the farm searching for mushrooms. Our finds were handed to the farmer's wife who also had a ruddy complexion, was slightly overweight and always wore her hair in a bun. Unlike her husband a smile very seldom appeared. It was rumoured that she had a fierce temper and often vented her spleen on her husband.

With the arrival of summer and school holidays most of our days were spent at the farm, the pinnacle of this activity being hay-making! The horse drawn cutting machine went backwards and forwards across each field causing numerous rabbits who used this as their refuge, to bolt, only to be quickly despatched by one of the labourers with a shotgun. A stick would be cut and a knife used to make an in insertion into one rear leg in front of the Achilles tendon. The other rear foot was then threaded through this incision and the resultant crossed legs threaded onto the stick that was later placed onto the shoulder and the total 'bag' taken back to the farm for distribution. Thirty to forty rabbits were not uncommon.

Within days of the cutting, and providing it had not rained, the next process was to scatter the grass to speed up the drying process. Again a horse-drawn 'scatter' was used; its large wire wheels (rather like circular grass rakes) would be driven up and down the lines of cut grass. The man controlling the horse sat on a large, shaped metal seat that was attached to the main machine by a long flat piece of metal some three inches wide and just under an inch thick. Due to its length it had a springing motion which gave a more comfortable ride. With this task completed and within a few dry days hay-making proper would begin. The men used hay forks. These were metal made into a long wide hoop culminating into two sharp points. The apex of the hoop was attached to a long wooden handle. These were thrust into the turned hay, hoisted into the air and thrown up into the attendant horse-drawn hay-cart. It had extra long inward-sloping sides, with one of the labourers standing within the cart directing and stacking the growing load. The air would be full of dust. Sweat ran down the faces of the men and soaked their collarless shirts. The highlight of all this effort was the arrival of the farmer's wife carrying large baskets laden with thick slices of home-baked bread, chunks of home-made cheese, apples and what everyone, including my friend and I, wanted and needed – lashings of hot sweet tea! Everyone would rest around the hay-cart to enjoy this simple and filling food. Within thirty minutes the leader would stand up. It was time to continue.

With the arrival of autumn two other events took place: rat catching and 'rabbiting'.

As any farmer will tell you, every farm is 'crawling' with rats and as they eat anything and spread disease, from time to time they have to be eradicated. These culls were conducted by 'professional' rat catchers. Their 'equipment' consisted of small nets that could be placed over any detected rat exit holes, and perhaps three ferrets and two to three terriers. Due to the number of buildings it was an all day job. The ferrets were placed down the holes causing the loosened terriers to bark with excitement. The nets were placed and the men stood by with shovels. At first all was quiet. Within minutes squealing could be heard. Suddenly rats appeared! Some were trapped by the nets to be despatched with a blow from a shovel. Those that escaped were quickly killed by the terriers. The ferrets would reappear and the whole process was repeated. There were always a few remaining survivors and this final hunt ensured their demise. Each building produced as many as thirty rats, their bodies later being buried in a large hole. The total bag for the day could exceed well in excess of one hundred rats!

The same men would later appear to carry out 'rabbiting'; the only change to their 'equipment' being shotguns in place of the terriers. As rabbits consumed growing crops (don't forget we were at war), rabbits provided a source of fresh meat, so 'rabbiting' was very popular within the local rural area. The system was almost the same. The ferrets were fed down the rabbit holes, the nets placed and held secure with a wooden peg. As before the men waited. Soon rabbits were being caught in the nets and killed by a blow on the back of the neck with a stick. Any that evaded the nets received their coup de grace with a shotgun. As per the 'hay-making rabbits' the crossed legs were threaded onto a pole. Being a spectator had its rewards as I was also given a rabbit to take home, which made a welcome addition to our meagre meat ration. Which reminds me. As rationing was in force, at the butcher's there was no question of choice – as a result you placed into your shopping basket what the butcher handed to you. My mother was fully convinced that as we were evacuees the butcher handed over the "scrag ends' (unpopular cuts of meat).

Whilst on the subject of meat, I should mention my goat. How this came about was the farm's goat gave birth to three kids, two being female and the other male. Now as female goats are milk producers the male kid's fate was sealed. He was for 'the chop' both physically and metaphorically. He was white and the thought of this small creature appearing on the dinner table caused me the 'odd' sleepless night. As a result I asked the farmer if I could have him. He smiled and looked down at me.

"Ter eat or ter keep as a pet?" He enquired.

"To keep as a pet!" I replied.

He shook his head. "Yer muther won't like it – goats are reet smelly buggers."

A sack was produced and with my newly acquired pet with his head sticking out I set off for home. Apart from the initial struggle inside the sack and a few bleats we arrived home without incident. I opened the front door.

"You'll never guess what I've been given!"

My mother and grandmother appeared from the kitchen.

"It's a goat!"

I had not considered the implications of having a goat as a pet and merely said,

"Isn't he beautiful?"

I released the string securing the goat's head in the neck of the sack.

"Just look at him."

Once released the tiny goat gave a small bleat, looked around and wandered into our tiny front lounge. There it spread its rear legs and a cascade of hot urine descended onto the rug which promptly soaked it up as the cascade spread. The response was immediate!

"You can't keep it here; you must take it back to the farm!"

By this time the goat was sniffing around and I had the distinct impression that lumps of unpleasantness were about to hit the rug! I quickly gathered up the goat and the sack and made for the door as a series of tiny lumps were left in our wake. As we had no garden and the goat wasn't house trained, despite my pleadings I had to place the goat back into the sack and with a heavy heart set off for the farm. Each time it looked at me I had visions of its ultimate – fate – the farmer's dinner table!

Some weeks later I was again at the farm to see one of the men carrying a small bag and heading for the large water trough. Arriving there he opened the bag and withdrew five or six tiny black and white kittens. He then proceeded to drop them into the trough two at a time and held them under the water. I was horrified! Looking down at the pair of drowning kittens I noted a stream of small bubbles emanating from their open mouths. When the bubbles ceased the pair were withdrawn from the trough and dumped onto the ground. He then picked up the next mewing pair. As he was about to drop them into the water he saw the expression on my face.

"Farm 'as too many cats so we 'ave ter git rid of 'em."

To my eyes this was stark cruelty!

"Can't they be given to good homes?" I asked.

He shook his head. "Nay who'd 'ave em?"

He looked at me. Do yer want wun?"

He held the hapless pair up by the scruff of their necks.

"Do yer fancy wun of these?"

I chose the one in his left hand took it from him and cradled the tiny creature in my arms. Not wishing to witness the fate of its companion, I set off for home with my newly acquired pet. Arriving at the front door I somehow knew that this time my pet would be accepted. And it was! I christened it 'Puss'. Being so tiny 'Puss' had to be spoon fed on warm milk and as the weeks progressed 'Puss' grew stronger and stronger, and his antics at the age of six to seven weeks, when trying to catch a twist of paper tied to a string, kept us all amused. With the passage of time 'Puss' started to deplete our domestic mice.

The canal ran past our house and access to the tow-path was via the small humped-back bridge that was on my route to school. At week-ends I would take 'Puss' with me when I went fishing for Gudgeon. These were about three-to-four inches long and were plentiful within the waters of the canal. My 'fishing rod' was a long thin stick acquired from the nearby wood. The line was a length of black cotton tied to the tip of the stick; the 'float', a piece of broken twig and the hook a bent pin. As per my previous fishing trips, the bait was supplied by worms found underneath nearby stones and then impaled on the bent pin 'hook'. 'Puss' would be beside me. The 'float' would disappear under the water. I would pull on the line and produce a wriggling three-to-four inch fish. This was 'donked' on the head and handed to 'Puss'. After a day's fishing, I would pick up 'Puss' (avoiding his distended stomach), then clutching my 'rod' set off for home. Only once did 'Puss' disgrace himself, as upon arrival home he was promptly sick on the kitchen floor. When we finally returned to Brighton, 'Puss' was handed on to Billy and no doubt either died of a 'ripe old age', or if his fish diet continued at its former level, from protein poisoning.

18.   Extra mural activities

Within the village (I refer to school aged children) there were two types of activity: legal and illegal. The latter referred to 'scrumping' (stealing apples from trees). I suppose that I should add another – being naughty. After several months I became friends with a boy who was in my class whom I would describe as 'Jack the Lad'. From time to time we would roam around the local countryside, make bows and arrows and the ultimate – catapults. He said that he was friendly with the village black-smith stating that, from this unlikely source, he could obtain metal pellets that were ideal for catapults. Together we visited the blacksmith who at that time was shaping metal hooves. When the shoe was red-hot it was placed underneath a large hand operated punch which formed the holes where nails could be inserted when shoeing a horse. These punch-holes produced square round ended metal pellets. The blacksmith was very friendly and was quite happy for the two of us to scoop up a hand-full of these discarded, and by now, cool punchings. The idea being that these would be ideal for shooting at rabbits, or even the 'odd' pheasant. As meat was rationed this seemed to be a splendid idea. Joining my companion we set out to search for two suitable Y branches that would form the basis of our catapults. Once found and cut to size the next requirement was quarter-inch square elastic. The leather that would hold the iron pellet could be fashioned from the tongue of a discarded boot or shoe. Within two days we had two catapults. I cannot recall from where we obtained the heavy-duty elastic, but it duly appeared. Thus armed, after school, if I was not at the farm, we would set off in search of rabbits. During the course of the next few weeks we fired scores of iron pellets. The result, apart from convincing future geologists that they had discovered an unusual source of iron ore, was a field devoid of rabbits. We had no hits whatsoever! What we did discover was that it was possible to 'walk' within fifteen paces of young rabbits before they would bolt for 'home'. The method was to take minute steps of no more than three inches. From time to time standing perfectly still with the catapult held across the body, the pellet in place and being held in situ between the thumb and fore- finger ready for action. If the rabbit looked up we 'froze' and as it commenced eating, then again move slowly forward.... Using this method with baby rabbits it was possible to get within ten paces. These tiny rabbits were not shot at.

It was late summer and yet again we were about to return home empty handed. We were passing very close to the farmer's orchard when my companion said,

"Do yer fancy summ apples?"

He inclined his head in the direction of the orchard.

"I can nip over t'wall. You keep watch."

With these words he scaled over the low stone wall and climbed into one of the trees. As he did so there was a yell from a female voice – it was the farmer's wife! My 'blood froze in my veins'! I had not been spotted, which was just as well as I would have been banned from the farm. With a muttered "bluddy 'ell", my colleague started to rapidly descend the tree as the farmer's wife arrived at the orchard. Escape was impossible, not due to the proximity of the farmer's wife, but a short stump had disappeared up one leg of his shorts, bringing his proposed escape to a shuddering halt. I heard the farmer's wife say,

"This is what I do ter thieving lads like you!"

I heard the clank of a bucket quickly followed by the sound of water being thrown plus a yell from my impaled companion. This was quickly followed by three more clanks, three sounds of water being thrown and a further three yells! I then heard what is best described as a wet whack! This also produced a yell! I was crouched behind the wall with my heart thudding in my chest. I then heard the farmer's wife say,

"If I catch yer here again I'll beat yer with a horse whip. Now git down and be off!"

I heard scrambling on the other side of the wall which was quickly followed by a wet clog and a soggy sock. He was crying and soaked from head to foot. We both ran towards home. I asked what had happened. Between tears he said,

"Bluudy branch went upp me shorts. She kept throwing buckets of water all over me and then 'it me on the backside with a stick. I'll 'ave a red mark theer fur days!"

Never again did he suggest that we went 'scrumping'. We continued to fire iron pellets at rabbits and always went home as usual, empty handed.

The canal, apart from providing me with the joys of fishing, and providing 'Puss' with a distended stomach, it also provided a source of leisure for the village. There were trips along the canal in a horse-drawn barge to the nearest town for a day out. How simple pleasures were in those days. The barge was normally used to transport cargo, but with the tarpaulin covers off it could accommodate about fifty people. As all the fit young men were in the Forces, the occupants consisted of mainly women and children, with a smattering of (to my eyes) old men. The horse can best be described as a 'cart-horse'. These were big powerful animals and were bedecked with the usual horse-collar and all the 'horse-brasses" were highly polished. A man sat astride the horse and his companion was on the tiller keeping the barge in the centre of the canal. With the fares collected, and the tow-rope some twenty yards long attached to the horse, we were off! Initially the horse strained on the rope and once we were under way from then on it appeared to be effortless. Above the excited voices of the children and the admonishments of their mothers not to lean over the sides, the steady 'clip-clop' of the horse's hooves on the tow-path added a soothing sound as we journeyed towards our destination. I can well recall the sunlight filtering through the trees that lined the canal bank causing deep shadows to be cast onto the tow-path and the canal, with shafts of sunlight flickering across our faces and highlighting the towpath and the adjoining fields.

There were two minor drawbacks. The sanitary arrangements were provided by two buckets: one in the forepeak for the women and children, the other in the stern for the men. As each 'toilet' had a head height of less than five feet, I leave the relevant scenarios to the reader's imagination. The other drawback was the horse. No doubt it had been well fed on oats and water prior to its exertions. When under way the horse would from time to time, produce a series of loud rude noises. Due to the forward motion of the barge, most of this cloud of odorous discharge descended upon the occupants, causing the ladies to rapidly waft their handkerchiefs underneath their noses, or to pinch their nostrils, until the sweet smelling country air could once again be drawn into the lungs. The man on the tiller seemed oblivious to the horse's fairly frequent 'offerings', and as he was grey haired and apparently fit, it proved that this 'country air' was not without its benefits.

At our destination the now excited and 'gassed' occupants of the barge made their various ways into the local town. We had just two hours to wander around the shops, drink the inevitable cups of tea, or for the children the Yorkshire 'brew', 'Dandelion & Burdock'. The return journey would have the ladies showing each other their various non-rationed bargains and no doubt hoping that the horse's gastric juices were now dormant. The children would run around within the confined space being constantly admonished by their mothers to either behave, or stop leaning over the side of the barge. In the warm days of summer such simple pleasures provided a welcome change to normal village life.

With summer now a fairly distant memory and the arrival of early darkness other nocturnal activities came into play. There were dances held at the social club, but as most of the young men were away women danced with women. Other social activities were held in the church hall, 'Beetle Drives' being very popular. This was not a search and destroy operation against an infestation of pests, but was conducted with a dice and everyone seated at tables. From memory, the dice were thrown. A six had to be obtained as this gave a start and allowed the participant to draw a circle (the beetle's body). It was five for a head, three for a tail two for each eye and one for each of the six legs. At the word "Go!" each dice was thrown as rapidly as possible, the deep sighs and frowns of concentration showing that elusive six was yet to be obtained. Within minutes someone would shout "Beetle!" Then go forward to receive their prize. During this brief interlude, the other participants would compare with their near neighbours their failed results. There would be numerous shakes of the head, many "tch tch" sounds. Then it was eyes down for the next round. Each prize was very basic, perhaps a donated loaf of homemade bread. Vegetables were also very popular prizes. As eggs were rationed and as some of the villagers kept chickens, half a dozen newly laid eggs would be the top prize for the evening. The Vicar was always in attendance and had the expression of a man swamped in pleasure. As it cost only tuppence (less than 2p in today's coinage) to participate, and there were about seventy to eighty parishioners in attendance, it helped to swell in a modest way, the church coffers.

The Girl Guides and the Boy Scouts gave concerts. These were always well supported, the Vicar opening each event with a brief prayer, reminding us that others were fighting for their country. The Guide Captain would then appear on the small stage and would announce in a semi-high voice – "The girls will now sing our camp fire song." She would beam at the audience through her steel-rimmed glasses, as the entire troop of some twenty girls, looking shy or waving at their families in the audience, would then shuffle onto the stage. As the troop were different ages and heights, to ensure that everyone fitted onto the small stage involved several changes of position. The Guide Captain would now face the girls and raise both hands into the air. The audience would fall silent. The Captain would scan her 'flock' and say -"Ready; one two three!" And the shrill voices would give their rendition of their camp-fire song, accompanied on an old upright piano, its heritage being denoted by the two brass candle holders affixed to its front and positioned either side of the music stand. Upon completion of the song, the Guide Captain would once again turn around, beam at the audience and make a small curtsy to thunderous applause! What followed were a series of mini plays, with the 'actresses' saying their stilted lines. The audience was in raptures and only once broke into unexpected laughter when one of the Guides said "fart" instead of "part." I cannot recall the dialogue, but at the time I could well understand how the error was made. The 'poor' girl must have been mortified. I was soon to discover she was not alone. These evenings ended with the National Anthem which was sung by one and all with gusto and fervour!

Prior to my arrival in the village my Aunt Hilda had given me an old wooden ukulele. The strings were tensioned with wooden keys and then tapped on the reverse side with a piece of wood to jam the keys in place. From time to time the keys would work loose and thus be out of tune. On this instrument I strummed 'Home on the Range' which was a popular cowboy song, plus several 'George Formby' numbers, (who was very popular at the time), my favourite being 'When I'm Cleaning Windows'. The lyrics were, I was later to discover, somewhat 'racy', but at that time words such as, "The bridegroom he is doing fine I'd rather have his job than mine" did not register. The Boy Scouts had heard of my musical 'ability' and invited me to appear in their show. I had a brief audition and looked forward to my debut. The concert followed similar lines to that of the Guides. The main difference being that the Scout Master wore shorts and knee length socks and not navy blue stockings. The one common factor was the 'woggle'. I digress. My turn was announced. My mother and grandmother were there to watch my debut – "Who knows" my grandmother said, "One day you might appear on the stage." However, her visions of my musical career were somewhat premature. I gave my bow and commenced to strum and sing 'Home on the Range'. Despite a previous check, one of the keys started to come loose. The result was a series of off key 'twangs'. I had to stop and tried to tune the ukulele with the same result. I could sense that the audience was becoming restless. The Scout Master came to my aid saying that I would try to repair the instrument and if successful I would appear again later. I never did and the ignominy of the incident lived with me for days. I was not approached to play at their next concert.

Village dances were always well attended and providing I was home by 9.00pm I was allowed to attend. I seem to recall that the entrance fee was sixpence (2.5p in today's coinage) for 'young people' and a shilling (5p) for adults. The 'band' consisted of just three grey-haired men. One played the piano, one on the drums and the final member on the violin, who normally doubled as 'master of ceremonies'. The dances were a mixture of traditional dances such as the 'barn dance' whereby the ladies were in a circle, the men (who were in short supply) forming the outer circle and in order to even the numbers were joined by some of the women. The music would start and the outer circle went clockwise, the inner one anti-clockwise. When the music stopped whoever was opposite you was your partner for the barn dance. At this stage of my life I was not overly tall and with some of the more rotund ladies, when holding them for the dance I was amazed to feel something like ironware beneath their dresses. These ladies also presented a problem. My nose was at bosom height! Which way was I to face in order to keep my nose from becoming entrapped in the fold of some enormous bosom? Dancing with young girls was much more pleasant. They were light on their feet, wore some kind of perfume, didn't have 'ironware', they didn't perspire, and didn't smell of a mixture of lavender and mothballs! The modern dances were the waltz and the 'quickstep'. The dances were interposed with the 'ladies excuse me' whereby a lady was permitted to approach a dancing couple and ask the female partner to let her continue with her male partner. There was also a male 'excuse me' session. I had to 'keep my eye on the clock' and always had to leave when things were 'going with a swing'.

As the weeks turned into months my circle of friends increased and now included the butcher's son. Bad language within the boys of my class at school was part of the lingua franca. "Bluudy 'ell!" was a common expletive and "A big bugger" was used to comment on the size of e.g. a horse or cow. One day the butcher's wife heard me swear and told her son he was never to play with me again! As he 'swore like a trooper', but obviously not at home, the lady assumed she was saving her son from the clutches of those bad evacuees.

One day I was asked by my mother to go an errand. In my newly acquired Yorkshire accent I replied "Bluudy 'ell mum do I 'ave ter go now?" Rather like the butcher's wife

I received a stern lecture about playing with one of the village boys. She said that Billy was a 'nice boy' (as you know he swore). Also the boy from London was placed into this angelic category

With early autumn fast approaching I joined a mixed group of boys and girls which included Billy, the boy from London and the butcher's son, plus Betty and Monica. From memory the group totalled about ten in number. We would roam on the nearby moors, walk along the canal tow-path towards the nearby town. We never arrived, the reason? On route there was much to divert our attention. At this stage our ages ranged from ten to eleven. On our way home we sat beside a small wood to rest when someone, I believe it was one of the girls, suggested that we should play 'truth, dare, or promise'. This was something new in my experience. The 'truths' ranged from "Do you like Jane?" To: "Is it true that you used the word "bluudy" today?" The 'dares' I will leave until later. 'Promises' ranged from helping in the home, to not swearing. The 'dares' at first were fairly innocent: for example. "I dare you to climb that tree." Or: "I dare you to kiss Betty". The girls were more accustomed to 'earthy' pursuits and having been in a huddle and having giggled several times, said to the butcher's son, who had chosen a 'dare'. "We dare you to show us your 'willie'." There was a brief pause and the appendage was produced with the girls giggling and turning away holding the hands over their mouths. The girls were then challenged to accept a 'dare'. Betty accepted and it will come as no surprise that she was 'dared' to show her 'willie'. She lifted her skirt and pulled down her navy blue knickers. I had never seen a naked girl before and I was amazed to see that it was an entirely different shape and a piece was missing! Billy leaned forward and went to either take a closer look, or touch it. Before he could do so, he was pushed away and the object of our gaze was quickly covered up.

Later Billy and I discussed this amazing difference, but apart from conjecture – Billy said he had been told this was where you 'put it', we failed to reach any firm conclusion. It was only some weeks later when at the farm and seeing a bull 'riding a cow', it appeared what Billy had been told could be true.

In the few remaining weeks of light evenings, we were to be shown other 'willies' including Monica's and the other girls. However, now that we knew that girls were different from boys, all interest in this area ceased. With the onset of winter nights and early darkness, all games outside of school hours came to a halt.

19. Our family at war

Soon after our arrival in Yorkshire my mother and Aunt Hilda had to report to be assessed for war work. My grandmother, due to her age, was exempt. The outcome was that my mother and Aunt Hilda were assigned to a munitions factory which was a bus ride away, to assist with the manufacture of cannon shells. Due to my age, my mother was selected to perform shift-work which was confined to daylight hours. Aunt Hilda being single was assigned to night-shift work. I had not realised that when we arrived in Yorkshire my mother was pregnant, so after several months she was discharged and from then on stayed at home. I was totally unaware of the actual reason. Being naive I had not even noticed her increasing figure. I was merely told that my mother didn't want to work at the factory and therefore had left.

With Aunt Hilda on constant night-shifts I realised that it was imperative she did not miss her bus. One day when my mother and grandmother were out I devised a method to arouse Aunt Hilda. It was a master plan! We could arouse her without anyone having to ascend the stairs. The sides of the staircase were boarded. Into the cream- painted boards I nailed a series of staples that led from the foot of the staircase to the top of the stairs, then left to outside her bedroom door. I threaded a string through the staples and, from the final staple, which was directly outside her door, I tied a hammer. Several jerks on the string from the base of the stairs produced a series of loud knocks as the hammer rose and fell. It was left in situ for Aunt Hilda to see and then I had to remove it.

The rationing system applied to nearly every foodstuff apart from the basics such as bread, cereals (porridge) and vegetables. Wild fruit grew in abundance in the hedgerows. In the autumn people were encouraged to pick wild rose hips as they were an excellent source of vitamin 'C'. With sugar rationed to just two ounces per person per week how could these wild fruits be stored? The solution was to convert this cornucopia not into jam, there was another method, 'bottling'. Glass 'Kilner' jars that would contain about two pints of fluid became very popular. These jars were washed, then sterilised in an heated oven. The fruit to be 'bottled' ranging from blackberries to plums and even tomatoes were preserved. Boiled water was poured onto the contents of the heated 'Kilner' jars and when cooled and stoppered with an air-tight glass lid, a rubber seal ensured that the jar was air-tight. Anyone owning chickens could store their eggs by smearing each egg in 'Vaseline' before placing them into a bucket of water. Freezing, as we know it today, did not exist. By resorting to these methods of preservation housewives now had a method to provide meals 'out of season'.

Fat was highly prized and any fat (known as 'dripping') was saved from any roasted or fried meat, which for the four of us weighed only eight ounces per week. 'Dripping' could be spread onto bread, used for frying and the brown residue that was underneath the solidified 'dripping' was a delicious addition to a slice of bread. 'Dripping' could also be used to make cakes and biscuits, but as the quantity was far less than our meagre meat ration could provide, cakes and biscuits were 'few and far between'.

The subject of biscuits reminds me of our first winter. It was bitterly cold and as all boys wore shorts, irrespective of the weather or time of the year, walking to and from school was a freezing experience. Arriving home, as we did not have any central heating (very few houses had this luxury), the only warm place was the kitchen where one of the gas stove's rings was kept alight on a very low setting. No doubt noting my 'frozen' face my grandmother asked if I would like a hot drink? At this stage of my life 'Ovaltine' topped the list, made with hot milk and a small spoonful of sugar. I sat at the large scrubbed wooden kitchen table as my grandmother opened the cupboard, and then placed two spoonfuls of 'Ovaltine' from its tin into a cup. She then added the sugar. As we waited for the milk to heat we talked of school. My grandmother mentioned a letter that she had received that morning from Uncle Tom. I should add at this stage my grandmother's large Victorian family had been ruled 'with a rod of iron'. These final words are very apt when I consider what was soon to follow. With the milk heated and poured into the cup, then stirred, I was handed this welcome 'defroster' by a benign and smiling grandmother. I held the cup in my cold hands enjoying its warmth and took my first mouthful – I spat it out all over grandmother's well scrubbed wooden table! This was not due to the heat – it tasted foul! As I had played tricks on my grandmother in the past, like nailing her slippers to the floor where they were kept just at the edge of the bed, her reaction was immediate! "You fiend!" Before I could explain my grandmother picked up what appeared to be a poker. Having experienced grandmother's wrath before, I was off my chair in a flash, ensuring that the table was between me and extinction. We both made several circuits, sometimes dodging 'this way and that'. As 'annihilation nearly caught me' I rapidly reversed direction! During these rapid circuits I was shouting – "It was horrible!" The response was not said with affection, it was "I'll give you horrible!" And the pursuit continued! After several more circuits and no doubt due to my grandmother's age, she stopped. The protection of the table ensured this brief interlude of safety. Despite her still raised 'poker' I managed to persuade her to try the 'Ovaltine'. She did so, 'pulled a face', smiled, placed the poker onto the table, came around to my side and gave me a kiss on my forehead. I was saved! So how could this 'Ovaltine' taste foul? There was a product on the market that was used to thicken gravy called 'Bisto'. Older readers may recall that it came in a thin cardboard packet and the 'logo' depicted a boy and a girl sniffing appreciatively at its aroma. As the packaging attracted moisture, my grandmother had placed the 'Bisto' powder into a discarded 'Ovaltine' tin. 'Bisto' mixed with hot milk and sugar nearly caused my early demise. Following the kiss, grandmother fumbled underneath her apron and from the cloth bag that was used to contain coinage, produced a sixpence. I cleaned the pristine table and domestic bliss returned once more.

Returning from school at lunch-time there was an air of excitement. Uncle Tom and Aunt Kit's bungalow in Polegate had been partly wrecked by a near miss from a German flying bomb. Evidently the windows had been blown in, a large quantity of roof tiles had disappeared, the bungalow's contents were damaged and covered in rubble. The result: Aunt Kit, my cousin Joan who was ten years older than myself, plus their dog, were on their way to stay with us! With only three tiny bedrooms sleeping arrangements would be, to say the least, cramped! What quickly went through my mind was how would the dog react to 'Puss'?

With the passage of time I cannot recall the sleeping arrangements, but with three adults in the house (Aunt Hilda on night-shift), plus myself, the addition of another adult and a teenage girl, not forgetting the dog, conditions would be very cramped. I can only assume that the small lounge (referred to as the front room), must have been converted into a bedroom. If we now consider the toilet and washing facilities (do not forget the galvanised bath), the family's normal standards of hygiene must have been under pressure. These arrangements overlook the fact that in the 1940's washing machines and dryers did not exist. Mondays was always set aside for wash-day. However, cotton bed-sheets alone took two days, with the kitchen being bedecked with dangling and drying bed-sheets. Clothes took another two days and I can recall the painted kitchen walls during winter, streaming with condensation. Solid metal irons were heated on the rings of the gas stove, the hot handles being held in several layers of cloth. As every bed-sheet was ironed, the laundry was never completed until Friday. My grandmother's method of testing the iron to ensure that it was at the correct temperature was achieved by first tapping the sole plate with a moistened finger. The resultant hiss was immediately followed by a slight nod of the head and the hot sole plate was then held close to her face. The iron was then quickly applied to a bed-sheet. I cannot recall ever seeing a scorched sheet.

The bathing arrangements (do not forget the galvanised bath), also absorbed a considerable number of hours. The water had to be heated in a number of large saucepans and for decorum I was always sent out to play with my friends. With the arrival of winter and early dark nights, no doubt I was sent to Billy's. I have omitted to mention that five saucepans of hot water emptied into a galvanised bath and the temperature adjusted with another saucepan of cold water provided a very shallow bath. Upon completion of one's ablutions, the bath was emptied by hand and poured down the old ceramic kitchen sink. To this day I cannot understand why we had left Brighton where we had a 'normal' bath and an inside toilet, for these primitive conditions almost defies belief! The threat of invasion no longer existed and Brighton was not a prime target. As I previously stated – so much for tea-leaves!

Aunt Kit's dog was a brown and white cocker-spaniel and the closest it ever came to aggression was wagging its short stumpy tail. Having advanced upon 'Puss' to take an inquisitive sniff, it was confronted with 'Puss' with every hackle raised, an arched back, a vertical tail and much hissing. Faced with this 'show of force', the dog decided to beat a hasty retreat. From then on if ever they met (which in our small abode was very frequently), the arched back and hissing resulted yet again in the dog's rapid retreat. Despite these initial confrontations, within weeks the dog would settle down in the kitchen to be joined by 'Puss', who often received licks of affection. Due to 'Puss's' small size, these 'big licks' often pushed 'Puss's head to one side. 'Puss' loved it! The eyes would be closed and the purring showed that this was sheer bliss!' When Aunt Kit and my cousin Joan and their dog finally departed, it was evident that 'Puss' felt the loss.

On reflection it was not surprising that Aunt Kit wanted to return home as soon as possible. The conditions within 'our' house were very cramped and the bathing arrangements primitive. Compared to Aunt Kit's and Uncle Tom's home, our temporary home in Yorkshire was 'a tip'. We had been shocked when we first saw the house. Aunt Kit must have been horrified!

So with the departure of Aunt Kit, my cousin Joan and their dog our routine returned to normal. At this stage I was blissfully unaware that an addition to our family was soon to arrive.

The village was touched with tragedy. A 'Wellington' bomber crashed onto the canal tow-path killing its Polish crew. The area was cordoned off for weeks as the remains of the wreckage were removed. With the cordon removed it was now possible to visit the scene of this tragic incident. To the boys of the village it had a fascination that was difficult to describe. It certainly wasn't morbid. Perhaps it was because this was the first time that evidence of war and its possible consequences was not listening to the wireless, this was stark reality.

I recall visiting the scene. Trees were splintered, there was evidence of fire and a strange and unpleasant smell lingered in the air. It was where six of our allied airmen had met their untimely death. We returned home along the canal, each of us saying little and we parted company without our usual banter.

It was soon after this incident that I saw the 'Home Guard' in 'action'. You will recall that past the school and over the wooden swing-bridge that crossed the canal, the road went up the hill. The large field (owned by the farm) was on its left. It was a Saturday and the field was occupied by about one hundred 'Home Guard'. Situated in the lower corner close to the road were some wooden tripods holding rifles. In the far top left-hand corner of the field at a range of some one hundred yards, were plywood figure targets. I stopped and leaned over the stone wall listening to one of the officers addressing some of the men. He was saying that they had to imagine a cross-wind was blowing and the rifles had to be adjusted to 'aim off for wind'. The men, many of them grey-haired, came forward one at a time, placed their shoulders to the rifle and pointing it at a figure target. Having done so, they stood back and adopted the 'at ease' position, feet apart and hands crossed behind the back. The officer then came forward, peered along the rifle, nodded his head as a sign of satisfaction, and then slapped the butt of the rifle to knock it out of alignment. The next man then came forward. I seem to recall that it was either the third or fourth man who repeatedly failed to receive the required nod of the head. The officer went to great lengths to repeat what was required. He then stood back. Again the man aligned the rifle and stepped back. The officer stepped forward, peered along the rifle, threw his hands in the air, ripped off his khaki forage cap, threw it onto the ground and proceeded to jump up and down on it – shouting "You're bloody miles away!" At this juncture I decided to continue up the hill towards the farm.

My next encounter with the 'Home Guard' was at the village fête. The ladies who attended the local church, had arranged several stalls displaying; used clothing; (remember, even clothes were rationed), the ever popular vegetable stall; another with home made ginger-beer and home made 'wines'. The 'wines' were nettle, parsnip and a pale pink 'wine' made from beetroot. As sugar was rationed, I can only assume that perhaps honey had been used in the production process. This stall was soon sold out! I refer to the 'wines' and not the ginger-beer. The other stalls that I can recall were the ever popular tombola, whereby every item (mostly unwanted crockery and other sundry items) were displayed. Each item was affixed with a stick-on raffle ticket. A large ceramic bowl held a pile of folded tickets and for a penny one could rummage around in the bowl, withdraw a folded ticket – and, if the number coincided with one on the 'cornucopia of 'goodies', walk away with a prize.

There was an atmosphere of happiness and goodwill. The flags and bunting fluttered in the warm afternoon breeze, as the Vicar, sporting a straw trilby hat, 'did the rounds' and projected a warm encompassing smile that all Vicars have on such occasions. Adding to this overall air of goodwill was music. This was provided by a hand-cranked gramophone – the music constantly stopping as the record ended with a scratching sound, quickly followed by silence. This lasted until the record (which was a 78 r.p.m. black Bakelite disc about twelve inches in diameter) was turned over and the gramophone rewound. It was important to place the small metal pin (known as a gramophone needle) into the groove of the record. The gramophone needle was attached to the gramophone's metal head. From there the sound was conveyed via a metal tube to a large metal horn to amplify the sound. However, in the open air, plus a light breeze, the sound was very little unless one was standing 'down-wind'. The gramophone was completely mechanical. In the 1940's this was almost the only method of playing music. We now come to the 'Home Guard'.

Spread onto a waterproof ground-sheet was an assortment of unloaded weaponry under the watchful eye of their uniformed guardians. (School-boys are attracted to weaponry like wasps to jam). These 'guardians' ensured that the exhibits were not handled by eager young hands, or 'disappeared". The 'pride of place' was held by the 'Spigot Mortar'. The mortar was very low in profile and the man firing it had to lie down behind a low metal shield in order to sight, and then fire the weapon. Projecting from the front of the mortar was what appeared to be a black metal rod some fifteen inches in length and about two inches in diameter. Over a hand-held megaphone (again non-electric), we were informed that a mortar bomb was about to be fitted onto the metal rod (spigot) and fired at a target on the canal bank some half a mile away. There was an audible gasp from the mainly female crowd. All eyes turned towards the canal where a figure in uniform was waving a large red flag. Beside him was a large oblong object.. Another 'Home Guard' stood beside the 'Spigot Mortar' also 'armed with a similar red flag. The moment had arrived! A mortar bomb some twenty inches in length, with a bulbous head with a metal shaft that culminated at four tail fins was then fitted onto the spigot. The 'Home Guard' in the prone position signalled that he was ready to fire. The man standing beside the mortar furiously waved his red flag. The man on the canal bank responded and was seen running away – the ladies with their 'screwed-up' faces held their hands to their ears. There was a tremendous BANG! The crowd gasped as the flight of the mortar bomb could be followed with the naked eye. It sailed up into the air in a large arc, rapidly descended and hit the target! The 'Home Guard' who had fired the mortar stood up, came to attention and saluted. There was a round of applause. The ladies commented to speak to each other about the incredible noise and the village boys, including me, gathered closer around the mortar coupled with lots of "Cors!" Soto voce "Bluudy 'ells", followed by much pushing and shoving in order to stand as close to the mortar as possible. The megaphone then announced that as the bomb was a practice round, the only damage to the canal bank was a score mark on the tow-path. Another demonstration was to follow! More bangs? We could hardly wait!

The man with the megaphone faced an expectant crowd of onlookers, noting that most of the boys had managed to work their way to the front in order to be as close as possible to whatever the 'Home Guard' planned for their next demonstration. Would it result in another huge BANG! It was noted that two of the 'Home Guard' were placing into a vertical position a sheet of metal some three feet long by about one foot wide and supporting it with wooden props. As they stood back a third 'Home Guard' approached and stood in front of the sheet of metal. In his hand he held what appeared to be a large 'plastic spherical lollipop' some six inches in diameter and protruding from its base a round black 'plastic stick' about nine inches long and about two inches in diameter. The announcer informed us that the 'lollipop' was a 'sticky bomb' and was used to destroy, or disable enemy tanks. The man with the bomb held it aloft for all to see, causing several of the female onlookers to 'screw up' their faces in anticipation and causing many of the boys to step closer, until they were ushered back into place by members of the 'Home Guard', assisted by our village police Constable. The man with the bomb took two paces closer to the crowd, causing the majority to step back – we (the boys) remained with expectant expressions. We were now informed that this bomb was live! There were a number of audible gasps from the mainly female crowd. The boys leaned forward in anticipation. The next announcement stated that the 'plastic' safety cover would be removed. Having done this the 'Home Guard' with the bomb once again held it aloft, and then removed from the base of the bomb (which the announcer said) was the safety pin. More gasps from the crowd as a 'Home Guard' and the police Constable with arm outspread contained the boys. At this stage we were informed that if this live bomb was mishandled the demonstrator could be killed! Several women in the crowd put a hand to their throats. However, the boys yet again had to be ushered back into place. What would happen? The 'Home Guard' with the bomb did a very smart 'about turn', whacked the bomb onto the sheet of metal, turned and ran about ten paces, then threw himself onto the ground. There was an enormous BANG! When I opened my eyes I saw that the bomb had blown a large hole in the metal. The demonstrator stood up, saluted, the crowd applauded and within seconds the gramophone commenced to play (with scratchy overtones) a song very popular at the time: 'They'll all ways be an England and England will be free, if England means as much to you as England means to me. Red white and blue what does it mean to you.........' The crowd took up the song and many of the women in the crowd had tears in their eyes, no doubt thinking of husbands and sons who were far away fighting for their country. The feeling of patriotic fervour was intense and I had a tingling feeling at the back of my neck as I joined in the song. The fête closed with an address by the Vicar, who reminded everyone present of the men who were at war and ended his address with a prayer, finishing with the 'Lord's Prayer' in which everyone joined. I can recall walking home with a feeling of intense pride – yes, there would always be an England!

20. An unusual surprise

It had been a bitterly cold winter. The canal had frozen and had been in this state for weeks. Ice formed on the inside windows of 'our' house and did not melt. The only warm room in the entire house was the kitchen, where one gas ring set on low heat maintained the whole house to just above freezing, this being achieved by leaving open all the interior doors. Visiting the outside toilet was a 'penance' – the seat was freezing! A small oil lantern placed below the overhead cistern (close-coupled toilets did not exist), stopped the uncovered pipe from freezing. It was against this background that my mother ceased working at the munitions factory. Harping back to my Polegate days, (as previously stated), my mother had maintained contact with my father – no doubt she had 'high hopes' that one day the three of us could become a normal family unit.

Christmas had come and gone. The snows still persisted and it was bitterly cold. To have my mother at home on a full-time basis was for me a bonus. At school a trick had been played on me that I thought was very amusing, so I decided to try this at home. As my mother went to sit down, I quickly pulled her chair away and she sat heavily onto the floor. My laughter was cut short. She started to cry and her face had drained of colour'. I helped her into her chair at the kitchen table as my grandmother appeared and I was sent to the front room. I realised that what I had done was serious, but little did I realise how serious until I was told to run and call the doctor. Luckily I had not caused any complications. My mother was confined to bed for several days and I received a very severe scolding from my grandmother and made to promise that I would never ever do anything like this in the future.

It was about this time when the snows once pure white and unsullied started to thaw. The ice on the canal took on a different colour and snowballs dripped with water. The air was still crisp and each breath produced a small cloud of vapour. I can recall those early mornings, looking across, still snow covered fields bathed in the light of a 'watery' sun and seeing the crows circling in the dull sky above the church-yard, their caws sounding sharp and raucous. At school it was good to feel the warmth of the classroom, no doubt added to by the many active bodies. So it was against this background that I was asked how I would like to have a baby brother or sister. I do not recall being overly enthusiastic. Both my mother and Aunt Hilda gave me 'pocket money'; I had a job at the farm and some very firm friends. Apart from these positive aspects, where would a baby sleep within our 'normal' domestic scene?

It was during late February that upon my return from school I was met at the front door by my grandmother. I was warned to be quiet, as my mother was asleep upstairs with my baby sister. I was told that when my mother awoke, then I could go and see her. About an hour later together with my grandmother, we ascended the stairs and carefully peeped into the bedroom. My mother was supported by two large pillows and cradled in her arms was a tiny red-faced baby. My grandmother whispered,

"This is your new baby sister, tip-toe over to the bed and have a look."

I did so and my mother held out one of her hands and gently pulled me towards the bed. She looked down at the baby and then at me.

"What do you think?"

I looked closely at the tiny red face. I cannot remember what I said, but I do recall not being very impressed. The baby's eyes were closed and it appeared to be fast asleep.

Within days it was apparent that all was not well. My grandmother, Aunt Hilda and my mother talked in low tones and the doctor was a frequent visitor to examine my new sister. Aunt Hilda remained at home spending most of her waking hours with the new baby. For my part school continued as usual. I can recall returning home one afternoon to find my grandmother looking very worried and Aunt Hilda had tears in her eyes. I was told not to go upstairs as my mother was nursing the baby. From snippets of conversation, it was apparent that my new sister was very ill and it was proposed that the Vicar should be called to baptise her. I have no recollection of the actual event, except being informed that the baby-bath was to be used as the font and that my sister's name was to be Patricia Evelyn. My sister survived her illness due I was informed, by Aunt Hilda's constant nursing.

As a result of my sister's arrival, bottles of concentrated orange juice, which came from America, arrived at 'our' house and from time to time I was allowed to mix this into a glass of water. The other aspect was that the Headmaster had heard all about the at home christening and as it was a Church of England school, we were 'lectured' on the need for this new arrival to be properly received into the church. During this 'lecture' 'all eyes were on me' and I can recall 'the terrible outcome' that awaited anyone who had not been properly baptised. This had little impact on me and as the orange-juice continued to arrive, I was still permitted, from time to time, to have a taste of this delectable juice; 'damnation' was soon forgotten.

My sister never was baptised in Church and I cannot imagine the Almighty saying: "You cannot ever enter here as you were baptised in a baby bath."

With my new sister fully recovered, it was pleasurable helping my mother to push the pram to the village Co-op, walk along the canal's tow-path, and generally 'take the air'. As my new sister was tiny it was possible to carry the lighter groceries inside the pram below my sister's feet. Each time the baby was fed I had to go into another room to occupy myself. Upon my return, my sister would be on the shoulder of either my mother, Aunt, or grandmother 'being burped'. It was amazing how much noise a tiny infant could produce!

It was during this time that I commenced producing toy soldiers. The normal pre-war soldiers made of lead were no longer obtainable so I resorted to clay that I obtained from another boy's garden. Each figure some three and a half inches in length was carefully fashioned and then baked in the ancient gas oven. When cooled any small cracks were filled with moist clay and when thoroughly dried, coloured with poster paints. I mixed the paints to produce a khaki colour for the uniforms and 'steel helmets'. Knapsacks, pouches and webbing I painted dark green. Boots were black. I tried to fashion faces but without success. I therefore resorted to 'faces' devoid of ears, noses and eyes, painting each 'face' in pale pink, which I also applied to the 'hands'. My initial trial efforts had not produced my imagined results. Prone figures did not present too many problems; it was the upright figures that were difficult. Being moist, when they were placed into the oven and the iron door closed, they keeled over and my production batch was misshapen. I tried propping each figure with very thin twigs – it will come as no surprise that these caught fire and the figures still keeled over.

What was I to do? My solution was a very low heat. The twigs didn't catch fire, each figure had less cracks and my collection commenced to grow. Billy and the evacuee from London were very impressed and decided to 'go into production'. Alas, this was before they suggested placing 'dirty' clay into an oven that was used to produce food. So my toy soldiers provided us with hours of enjoyment as we shouted out orders to attack, accompanied by a variety of vocal noises to represent guns, machine guns and shells, including the essential whistling noise as each shell was 'fired'. Any 'injuries sustained in 'battle' were soon repaired with a combination of moist clay, our oven and poster paint.

You will recall that Billy, the boy from London, and I lived beside the canal, so that apart from fishing, provided another source of enjoyment – sailing boats! We obtained some old off-cuts of timber and armed with a chopper supplied by Billy's mother (without her knowledge), plus an old kitchen knife obtained by the same means, we spent days shaping the hulls. A later trial revealed that each craft, some fifteen inches long, immediately flopped onto their sides – this was before we had fashioned the masts, sails and rigging. We needed metal keels to stabilise each hull. Being wartime metal of any sort was in short supply. Billy found the solution. He produced an old rusty piece of cast-iron. Careful examination, followed by consultation, we were of the opinion that it would make three keels. The cast-iron was about a quarter-of-an-inch thick. The solution was to hit it with a hammer in such a way that it would break into three pieces. It did! However, the end result did not produce three equal pieces. As it was Billy's iron he had first choice and chose the largest piece, the other two were not so dissimilar in size, so we were well pleased with the final outcome. Now, having a piece of irregular-shaped cast-iron for a keel was one thing, how could we attach these to the hulls? Over a period of days we fashioned slots into which to insert our now highly prized 'keels'. It was not easy and I must admit these slots were fashioned not without the 'odd' expletive. After 'a fashion' it 'worked'. We discovered that the wetted hulls swelled and gripped the 'keels'. With crude masts and booms fashioned from thin newly cut sticks, and sails made from various pieces of material, our fleet was ready to set sail. Beside the wooden swing-bridge and beside the London boy's home was the ideal place. The canal was not overly wide and with the swing-bridge it was possible to set the sails, run across the bridge and catch our craft before they reached the opposite bank. Only passing barges intruded into our hours of enjoyment.

With the onset of autumn evenings it was evident that sailing would have to cease. It was using a torch that gave me the idea of having a light on board, thus enabling us to keep track of our sailing craft. The reason for this was, although the sails were set to ensure that our 'models' merely crossed the canal, sometimes the wind would change and instead of crossing the canal, from time to time they would sail along the canal. As access points were limited, if our 'models' came to rest on the same bank as the launch point, retrieval was easy. However, coming to rest a hundred yards away on the opposite bank was 'another story'. So attaching a torch battery to the deck and a torch bulb as the base of the mast, connected by crude wiring, our night sailing began. Our efforts were short lived. All three households were adamant – night sailing was dangerous! What if one of us fell into the canal? So my precious and highly prized 'model' had to go into storage.

Several weeks later Billy asked me to come and see the boat his Uncle was making. His Uncle was excused active service and worked with metal. He had produced a metal hull some two feet long, each strip of thin metal was riveted to the adjoining strip. It was unfinished at the time, but without any doubt, this was a real model! I never did see the finished boat, but we all agreed that in the spring it would really sail! Alas, before the launch day, our family returned to Brighton.

21.   Travels to 'another world'

At this juncture a new element entered my life – travels into Lancashire! My Aunt Rhoda (who was considered to be the intelligent member of the family) was appointed to the position of Probation Officer in a large town within Lancashire. Her letter arrived and in it my Aunt suggested that during school holidays I may like to visit her. When this information was conveyed to me I readily agreed. As we were in Yorkshire and in order to reach this 'haven of expectation' I would have to change onto three different busses. My Aunt provided a typed letter addressed to the Senior Police Officers of Yorkshire and Lancashire requesting them to render me every assistance possible, should I become lost on route. I was instructed to present this letter immediately to any policeman in the event of (a) being unsure of which bus to catch; (b) feeling frightened by anyone on route; and, (c) becoming lost. Her letter to my mother contained detailed instructions regarding the specific route, which towns to ask for and the numbers of the buses per leg of the route. Arriving at my destination I was to telephone my Aunt and she would arrange for my collection. Thus at the first opportunity, I was off!

Prior to my departure I was placed into our kitchen tin-bath; avoided a visit to the village 'barber'; had several changes of my 'best clothes' packed into a small suitcase; had my shoes polished; been warned not to speak to strangers on route. Finally, not to hesitate to approach any policeman in the event of (a),(b) or (c). My mother escorted me to the local bus-stop where my mother reiterated my Aunt's letter to the Senior Police Officers in the event of (a),(b) or (c), and not to lose my ticket money. Finally, did I have the obligatory carefully ironed and folded white handkerchief in the right-hand pocket of my 'best' grey flannel shorts? Having boarded the local double-decker bus and having sat by the window, we both waived until we each disappeared from sight.

I was not accosted by strangers, found the 'Bus Inspectors' at each arrival point very helpful, and had no cause to produce my letter. I was met, hugged, then taken to my 'Aunt's house'.

The house was situated within an affluent part of the town and faced onto a major road that rose gradually from the town centre. It was large and imposing, which emphasised the smallness and run-down appearance of 'our' evacuee dwelling. The house was not owned by my Aunt but 'came with the job'. I was to quickly discover that it was used as a temporary remand centre for wayward girls who were waiting to appear before the local Court. My Aunt had a Matron to assist her and this lady's job was to be in charge of all domestic arrangements, which included strict supervision of the girls and organising their daily duties. It was at this address that I fell in love. Assisting the Matron was (to my eyes) a very beautiful young girl aged about seventeen. Evidently she had left home for a reason that my Aunt did not wish to discuss, and to my utter delight, I could be with her for the whole of my stay!

As the house was a temporary remand centre, every exterior door was double locked and every window, including those on the first floor, could only be partially opened. From time to time a police car would appear to convey some of the girls to Court. My Aunt, as the Probation Officer, normally accompanied them. Some of the girls did not return. Those that did had been remanded to some future date. The girls ranged in age from

circa sixteen to nineteen and during my stays were well be-
haved. I recall my Aunt saying that one of the girls escaped from
a Remand Home, hitch-hiked back to 'my Aunt's house' and
awoke her in the middle of the night requesting to be let back
in. My Aunt had to report this and the girl was sobbing as the
police arrived to collect her.

Being a young boy surrounded by about twelve girls, 'the love
of my life' and a Matron, I was more than spoiled. I did not find
being confined 'within four walls' onerous and there was always
plenty of young female company with whom to play 'draughts',
'Ludo' and other similar pastimes. From time to time I would
accompany my Aunt on her 'rounds', which no doubt were
carefully selected. I can recall that prior to one visit my Aunt
said I would be shocked at what I would see but I was not to
show any reaction. The dwelling was in a very poor part of town.
The young woman we were to visit lived on the first floor in one
single room. As we ascended the cracked and dirty linoleum
staircase there was a smell of urine. My Aunt knocked on a door
and it was opened by a girl aged about twenty who was holding
a child aged about two. The child had a 'runny' nose. To my eyes
they both looked unkempt. As we entered, the only furniture in
the room was a double bed with a stained pink mattress, a small
side table on which were two jam-jars; these were being used as
mugs. A solitary wooden chair was the only other item of
furniture. The floorboards were bare wood and like the bed
heavily stained. On the mattress was a small baby crying. The
whole room stank of urine. I had never before or since seen
squalor like this. Later my Aunt said the girl was subject to a
'Probation Order' and following my initial question I did not
pursue the cause.

I visited 'my 'Aunt's house' only twice and on my second visit the 'love of my life' had left. Evidently my Aunt had obtained a position for her as an Assistant Matron in some boys' private school. I have no doubt that they, like me, would soon be smitten.

So these two visits to my Aunt provided a welcome break from the confines of 'my' Yorkshire village and exposed me to both the 'upside' and 'downside' of life. Despite our poor surroundings within 'our' evacuee house, I realised how lucky I was to have such a loving and caring family.

Before the war my Aunt had occupied a similar position within some large town in the south-west of England. One summer my mother and I visited her as part of our holiday. Two things stand out in my mind: a girl, or should I say woman, who was named Bertha. The other was the 'resident ghost'. We had no fore-warning of either situation. Bertha 'lived in' and carried out general household chores. When not working she played with me in the large rear garden. Being very young, being chased was an all-time favourite. Bertha being fleet-of-foot always caught me. However, having been in situ for several days, I overheard my Aunt discussing Bertha with my mother. The following words 'sent a chill down my spine'. "Bertha is a lovely girl and as she has fits no one will employ her. The last time she had a fit, it took three policemen to hold her down." From then on every time Bertha suggested that we play 'chase' I always found some excuse not to do so. One day I was alone in the garden when Bertha suddenly appeared saying "I'll catch you!" With the picture of three burly policemen trying to hold her down, 'fear gave me wings' and I was off, finally ending up in my Aunt's office for protection. Evidently Bertha was never violent and having been thus assured, our games of 'chase' continued at a much gentler pace.

Let us now return to the ghost! The day we arrived and having been shown to our bedroom, my Aunt remarked – "If during the night you hear creaking on the stairs, don't be alarmed, it's our resident ghost." For the initial few nights I joined my mother in her bed and we clung to each other 'like limpets'! We never did hear any creaks on the stairs and with the arrival of sleep, then daylight, my heartbeat returned to normal. Having said this, I thought the dark wooden staircase and carpet, with its brass stair-rods looked 'spooky' and whenever possible I tried to avoid it when on my own.

I digress. It was soon after my second visit to my 'northern' Aunt that the family, now increased by one, decided that our living conditions left much to be desired. As a result we would return to the South. I have no idea if my grandmother 'consulted' the tea leaves, but with winter a distant memory we commenced to 'pack our bags'. Once again Aunt Hilda was despatched ahead of our departure date. Based on our original departure from Brighton, once again I had visions of piles of luggage, plus a pram to impede our progress This time there was a 'bonus', on arrival we would not be 'leapfrogging' to our front door.

How would I be received at school? I realised that once again my Yorkshire accent would be subject to ridicule and, despite my mother having my book which was awarded for being 'top of the school', a school that had only two teachers and about one hundred pupils would carry very little weight. I was right. This time I lasted just two weeks in the 'A' stream. It would be 'a long uphill struggle' before I entered the doors of the Grammar school. For this I have to thank my mother. Due to her persistence I was allowed to take 'a late entrance' examination. Following an interview with the local education department I was in! Within days of commencing my new academic career, it was very obvious that my peer group were 'way ahead of me' – it would take nearly a year to achieve a similar ability. It was going to be yet again, 'tough going' before I would be awarded my School Certificate.

Epilogue

Looking back over the years, despite the threat of invasion, I wonder if being evacuated to Yorkshire was the right choice, as we lived on the South coast and the Germans could use the beaches to spearhead their invasion. From my mother's point of view, knowing that I would not be engulfed in this expected invasion, the answer has to be an emphatic "yes." For my education in two small village schools, it was a near disaster. From an experience point of view, Nellie, Harold with his rabbits and chickens, plus their son Jack, has left me with a host of very fond memories. I still smile to myself as I recall Harold 'having trouble with his feet' and Nellie's reaction as he tried to hand over his packet of squashed sandwiches. Then there were the friendships that I developed within both villages. Another memory is my experiences as a choir-boy, singing carols as the snow 'scrunched' beneath our feet. The church bedecked with the 'goodness of the land' at each Harvest Festival. Last, but not least, the enjoyment of being 'a farmer's boy', Hay-making, 'rabbiting', my goat and my feline fishing companion, 'Puss'.

Why didn't I join the choir in the other Yorkshire village? Perhaps 'being a farmer's boy' had a lure that was difficult to resist.

Upon my final return to Brighton again I was to struggle with a curriculum that was 'beyond my ken'. It is thanks to my mother's persistence that I was allowed to take 'a late entrance' examination and thus qualify to enter the Grammar School where again I faced another new curriculum. It was a very proud moment for my mother when some years later a letter arrived stating that, having passed seven subjects I had been awarded my 'School Certificate'. Without this 'piece of paper' many 'doors would have remained closed'.

Six years later I would be in Kenya, East Africa when during the following ten years as a Colonial Police Officer it would provide another host of experiences – some 'hair-raising', some very humorous – memories of tracking Masai stock thieves, sleeping in the open in lion country with only our camouflage smocks as 'protection'; meeting my wife to be, Pauline, on the steps of Divisional Police Headquarters; the birth of our son Michael and later our daughter, Fiona. Now nearly sixty years later, some nights before I sleep, in my mind's eye I can picture it all so very clearly as these memories come flooding back. And Kenya? That's another story!

Alastair Tompkins
Crowthorne, Berkshire
November 2013